How to use your Snap R

This 'The History Boys' Snap Revision Text Gui⋯⋯⋯⋯⋯⋯⋯ r
AQA English Literature exam. It is divided int⋯⋯⋯⋯⋯⋯⋯⋯ ly
find help for the bits you find tricky. This boo⋯⋯⋯⋯⋯⋯⋯
know for the exam:

Plot: what happens in the play?

Setting and Context: what periods, places, events and attitudes are relevant to understanding the play?

Characters: who are the main characters, how are they presented, and how do they change?

Themes: what ideas does the author explore in the play, and how are they shown?

The Exam: what kinds of question will come up in your exam, and how can you get top marks?

To help you get ready for your exam, each two-page topic includes the following key information:

Key Quotations to Learn
Short quotations to memorise that will allow you to analyse in the exam and boost your grade.

Summary
A recap of the most important points covered in the topic.

Sample Analysis
An example of the kind of analysis that the examiner will be looking for.

Quick Test
A quick-fire test to check you can remember the main points from the topic.

Exam Practice
A short writing task so you can practise applying what you've covered in the topic.

Glossary
A handy list of words you will find useful when revising 'The History Boys' with easy-to-understand definitions.

**AUTHOR:
CHARLOTTE
WOOLLEY**

ebook

To access the ebook version of this
Snap Revision Text Guide, visit
collins.co.uk/ebooks
and follow the step-by-step instructions.

Published by Collins
An imprint of HarperCollins*Publishers*
1 London Bridge Street
London SE1 9GF

© HarperCollins*Publishers* Limited 2017

ISBN 9780008247171

First published 2017

10 9 8 7 6 5 4 3 2

British Library Cataloguing in Publication Data.

A CIP record of this book is available from the
British Library.

Printed and bound by CPI Group (UK) Ltd, Croydon, CR0 4YY

Commissioning Editor: Gillian Bowman
Managing Editor: Craig Balfour
Author: Charlotte Woolley
Copyeditor: David Christie
Proofreaders: Jill Laidlaw and Louise Robb
Project management and typesetting:
  Mark Steward
Cover designers: Kneath Associates and
  Sarah Duxbury
Production: Natalia Rebow

ACKNOWLEDGEMENTS

Quotations from *The History Boys* by Alan
Bennett © *The History Boys*, Alan Bennett,
Faber and Faber Ltd.

The author and publisher are grateful to the
copyright holders for permission to use quoted
materials and images.

Every effort has been made to trace copyright
holders and obtain their permission for the use of
copyright material. The author and publisher will
gladly receive information enabling them to rectify
any error or omission in subsequent editions. All
facts are correct at time of going to press.

MIX
Paper from
responsible source
FSC™ C007454

This book is produced from independently
certified FSC™ paper to ensure responsible
forest management.

For more information visit:
www.harpercollins.co.uk/green

Contents

Act 1 (part 1)

You must be able to: explore how the characters and themes are established at the start of Act 1.

What happens at the start of the play?

Several boys have passed their A-Levels and returned for Oxbridge exam lessons. Their teachers – Mrs Lintott (History) and Hector (English, General Studies) are joined by Irwin, to teach 'polish'. Hector's teaching is **flamboyant** and **esoteric** – but perhaps useless. Irwin insists they need more than accuracy to compete.

How does Bennett show different interpretations of education?

A significant conflict is over presentation, or letting ideas speak for themselves, as well as the purpose of education. The Headmaster is **elitist** and worried about league tables. Mrs Lintott says she doesn't distinguish 'between centres of higher learning' and that the boys will do well at other universities. The Headmaster asks for 'grooming' and 'the facts: serving suggestion'; Mrs Lintott has taught them thoroughly but plainly.

How does Bennett introduce the characters of Irwin and Hector?

The teachers' introductions show their different characters. Hector wears motorcycle leathers, which the boys take off and label in French – an odd activity but one which both **foreshadows** their unusual relationship and demonstrates their affection for him – in a way that might make audiences initially slightly uncomfortable in its familiarity. While Hector is 'fifty or so', Scripps describes Irwin as 'a new boy'; the Headmaster tells him to 'grow a moustache', highlighting his comparative youth.

In Hector's lesson, the boys act, in French, a scene set in a brothel that becomes a First World War medical centre when the Headmaster walks in. The scene is both absurd and the audience might consider it inappropriately sexualised for a classroom environment, but the **physical comedy** is entertaining to watch, as well as the bemused Headmaster. Irwin's lesson is a physical contrast, but Irwin also throws essays back and criticises their style.

What can we tell about the boys' relationships at the start of the play?

The boys are a tight group, often **sarcastic** – 'I know tradition requires it of the eccentric teacher, but would you mind not throwing the books?' They are affectionate towards Hector, demonstrated by the way they protect him from the Headmaster in the French scene. Following Irwin's lesson, they discuss their developing sex lives, and reveal Hector gropes them: 'think he thought he'd got me going but it was my Tudor Economic Documents'. This revelation might be shocking to an audience but the boys' matter-of-fact tone implies they do not experience discomfort over his actions.

Summary

- Beginning with Irwin in a wheelchair, the play flashes back to Hector.
- The boys have returned, post A-Level, for tuition to pass Oxbridge exams.
- The teachers have different views on education's value, and facts versus presentation.
- Hector has an eccentric teaching style and inappropriate relationship with the boys.
- Irwin is young, and is there to provide polish.

Questions

QUICK TEST
1. What are the main ideas about education in the opening scenes?
2. What views do Mrs Lintott and the Headmaster hold?
3. What kind of character is Dakin?
4. What are the relationships between the boys and their teachers?

EXAM PRACTICE
Using one or more of the 'Key Quotations to Learn', write a paragraph analysing how Bennett presents different ideas about education in Act 1, Part 1.

You must be able to: understand how Bennett develops his themes through Act 1.

How do Irwin's lessons progress?

Discussing recent essays on the First World War, Irwin tells the boys to look for 'an angle' and say something unexpected. Despite their wide-ranging knowledge, they recite the accepted teaching – that the First World War led to the Second World War. Irwin tells them that their answers will get them into other universities, but bore Oxford dons who want something unusual.

He tells them alternative interpretations, and argues that they need to look beyond the expected ideas. Scripps comments to the audience that later, when Irwin becomes famous, he demonstrated that the Americans were responsible for the Pearl Harbour attack.

Irwin instructs them on exam technique – find a question they can answer no matter what they're asked.

What is Hector's attitude towards literature?

The boys complain that they don't always understand poetry; Hector replies that they will, one day, when they have a corresponding experience that illuminates it.

He demonstrates the boys' wide-ranging knowledge when there's a knock on the door, discussing knocks in literature and **idiom**, but doesn't answer it.

How does the conflict over education and culture develop?

When the boys recite Larkin and Auden, Irwin tells them to use their knowledge in the exam. The boys (semi-teasing) tell him that they couldn't possibly use Hector's teachings: he's teaching them for life, not the exams, and the two concepts shouldn't cross paths.

Rudge tells Mrs Lintott that he misses the clarity of facts in her lessons, but while she taught them plainly they are 'acquiring flavour' with Irwin.

How do the boys' relationships change?

Dakin brags to Scripps that Fiona is his 'Western Front', and they discuss his sexual progress with her. To Posner, suffering unrequited love for Dakin, this is torturous. Although Scripps is sympathetic to him, he says it will pass with time.

The boys tease Irwin with their knowledge, telling him they won't use it in an exam, although Posner says they're 'taking the piss'. When he asks why he teaches with the door locked, they know it's an awkward question and respond with jokes: against 'the forces of progress ... the spectre of modernity'.

Key Quotations to Learn

Scripps: 'But it's all true.'

Irwin: 'What has that got to do with it? What has that got to do with anything?'

Hector: '... then you will have the antidote ready! Grief. Happiness. Even when you're dying. We're making your deathbeds here, boys.'

Rudge: 'You've force-fed us the facts; now we're in the process of running around acquiring flavour.'

Irwin: 'The wrong end of the stick is the right one. A question has a front door and a back door.'

Akthar: 'It's not education. It's culture.'

Summary

- Irwin tells them their essays are dull – they don't need truth, they need interpretation.
- Dakin's dating the Headmaster's secretary Fiona.
- Hector teaches with the door shut using a knock as an opportunity to explore connections in literature.
- Rudge misses the clarity of Mrs Lintott's lessons.
- Irwin encourages the boys to use Hector's teachings in his lessons but they view this as virtually **sacrilegious**.

Questions

QUICK TEST
1. What does Irwin tell the boys to study?
2. What does Rudge think of Irwin's lessons?
3. What is Hector's reason for teaching poetry in this section?
4. What do we learn about Dakin's relationships?
5. How does Irwin respond to the boys' literary and cultural knowledge?

EXAM PRACTICE
Using one or more of the 'Key Quotations to Learn', write a paragraph explaining the developing **conflict** between Irwin and Hector's philosophies of education.

Act 1 (part 3)

You must be able to: understand what happens at the end of Act 1.

How do Posner and Scripps express the difficulties of growing up?

Posner tells Irwin he's gay, and loves Dakin. Scripps, in an **aside**, says that all he wanted was some company and understanding. Posner didn't ask Hector because he'd have simply given him a quotation.

Scripps tells Dakin about his religious feelings, comparing it to being in love with God – something to get over with while young so he can move on, like Posner's **unrequited** love.

How has Dakin changed?

Dakin says he finds literature 'lowering', and that since meeting Irwin he's changed ideas. He's realised art and literature can be questioned.

There's an element of hero worship. When Dakin realises he said 'Kneeshaw' instead of 'Nietzsche' (pronounced 'nee-chuh') to Irwin, he's angry as he thinks Irwin will think him a fool.

How do Irwin and Hector clash?

Irwin wants Hector to tell the boys to use the literature they've learned with him. Irwin calls them 'gobbets', which offends Hector as being dismissive of literature. Rather than a handy punctuating conclusion, Hector argues the quotations are learned 'by heart' and should stay there. 'By heart' for Hector doesn't simply mean being able to recite, but being able to love the ideas encompassed in the quotations and to find emotional solace in them

How is Hector discovered?

The Headmaster summons Hector. The Headmaster's wife, volunteering at a charity shop, looked out of the window and saw Hector on a motorbike groping a boy behind him.

The Headmaster tells Hector he should consider retiring early. Hector replies with a quotation, frustrating the Headmaster. Hector tries to excuse his behaviour. Further angered, the Headmaster swears at him, and tells him that he has to share lessons with Irwin.

How does Hector's relationship with Posner develop?

Posner recites *Drummer Hodge* by heart to Hector, who tells him the drummer was his age, and Hardy about Hector's. Hector considers the use of the **prefix** 'un', creating a sense of melancholy: 'Un-kissed. Un-rejoicing. Un-confessed. Un-embraced'.

Echoing Posner's earlier concerns, Hector says the best moments in reading are when you recognise yourself in someone else's work. Hector reaches out, and it seems he'll touch Posner's knee, but then the moment is gone and Dakin arrives for a lift. Hector declines, leaving on his own.

Key Quotations to Learn

Hector: 'I count examinations, even for Oxford and Cambridge, as the enemy of education.'

Mrs Lintott: 'One of the hardest things for boys to learn is that a teacher is human. One of the hardest things for a teacher to learn is not to try and tell them.'

Irwin: 'Education isn't something for when they're old and grey and sitting by the fire. It's for now.'

Summary

- Posner tells Irwin he's gay.
- Dakin tells Scripps how much he admires Irwin for changing his world-view.
- The Headmaster has discovered Hector's 'fiddling'. He now must share lessons with Irwin.
- Hector and Posner read *Drummer Hodge* together.

Questions

QUICK TEST
1. Why does Posner confide in Irwin?
2. What does Dakin say about Irwin?
3. How is Hector discovered?
4. What's the Headmaster's response?
5. What happens between Hector and Posner?

EXAM PRACTICE
Using one or more of the 'Key Quotations to Learn', write a paragraph analysing the way Bennett creates a **melancholy** mood at the end of Act 1.

Act 2 (part 1)

You must be able to: understand what happens at the beginning of Act 2.

How does Bennett use time-shifts at the opening of the act?

Irwin, in a wheelchair, is filming at Rievaulx Abbey. He's 'five years older' in the **stage directions**. The audience now knows his accident must have happened soon after the events seen already.

A 'Man' appears, soon revealed as Posner. He has dropped out of Cambridge and is undergoing therapy. He's sold a story about Irwin and wants a quote. Irwin refuses to speak further.

At the scene's transition, Bennett uses the director's objection to the word 'apotheosis' to shift the scene, with Posner offering a definition to Hector in the classroom.

What happens to Hector?

When he says he's sharing lessons with Irwin, the boys tease him about their contrasting styles. Frustrated at their lack of seriousness and his situation, he breaks down and cries. The boys don't know how to respond to this unexpected emotion. Posner awkwardly rubs his shoulder. He rallies, and they act out a scene before leaving him alone at the desk.

What do Hector's colleagues think of his teaching?

The Headmaster says at least Hector's groping he can quantify and act on, whereas Hector's teaching is too unpredictable. Speaking to Irwin, Mrs Lintott admits she doesn't think Hector is that good. He has a 'well-meaning' attitude but treats education as insurance against failure. She calls him 'twat, twat, twat', a line either delivered to Irwin or as an aside to the audience, in her 'inner voice'.

What are the arguments for and against teaching the Holocaust?

At the start of their first shared lesson, Irwin suggests discussing the Holocaust.

Dakin suggests the Holocaust should be put into proportion. That goes too far for Irwin, who warns him not to call Hitler a 'statesman' and argues that Dakin's approach isn't true; Scripps points out he's told them all along that truth is subjective.

Posner, who's Jewish, argues that the atrocity should be discussed as such, and Hector agrees.

Irwin counter-argues that the historian's job is to create distance, to anticipate what the future perspective of the recent past will be.

Dakin tells Scripps that he knows Hector is leaving because someone knows about Hector's fondling.

Key Quotations to Learn

Headmaster: 'It isn't that he doesn't produce results. He does. But they are unpredictable and unquantifiable ...'

Mrs Lintott: '... what's all this learning by heart for, except as some sort of insurance against the boys' ultimate failure?'

Irwin: 'I don't think it's true, for a start ...'

Scripps: 'But what has truth got to do with it? I thought that we'd already decided that for the purposes of this examination truth is, if not an irrelevance, then so relative as just to amount to another point of view.'

Summary

- Irwin, five years older and in a wheelchair, speaks to an at-first unidentified Posner.
- Hector breaks down and cries in front of the boys.
- The Headmaster tells Mrs Lintott that Hector is leaving, and she admits that, although she likes him, she isn't sure that he is a good teacher.
- The boys, Irwin and Hector discuss the appropriate response to teaching the Holocaust.

Questions

QUICK TEST
1. Who is the 'Man' that speaks to Irwin?
2. How do the boys respond when Hector cries?
3. What does Mrs Lintott think of Hector's teaching?
4. How similar are Hector and Irwin in their views on teaching the Holocaust?

EXAM PRACTICE
Using one or more of the 'Key Quotations to Learn', write a paragraph analysing the way Bennett explores ideas about failure at the opening of Act 2.

You must be able to: understand what happens in the middle of Act 2.

What happens with Posner's parents?

They complain to the Headmaster, who is angry with Irwin for potentially making the school look like it hires Holocaust deniers, and instructs him to apologise. Speaking to Posner, Irwin admits he was too dispassionate but isn't really apologetic.

How do the boys discuss sex?

Dakin has 'broke[n] through' Fiona's Western Front. Posner asks if he's afraid it's all going to be over too soon – a fundamental difference between them as Dakin's carefree response is 'you can't save it up'. Dakin also wonders if he might sleep with Irwin.

Posner tells Scripps that Irwin does like Dakin: their eyes meet over him.

How are the mock interviews conducted?

The three main teachers interview the boys, offering suggestions for improvements to their answers. Even Mrs Lintott agrees some presentation is required telling Rudge 'I like film' is better than liking 'films', implying it's more intellectual.

Irwin also tells the boys to adapt their answers but Hector insists they should tell the truth.

The boys remain sarcastic and witty, except Rudge, who says history is 'one fucking thing after another', and who insists that if they want to take him they will because he's interesting enough and good at sports.

How does Mrs Lintott's feminism come through?

Telling the boys they may be interviewed by a woman, she says how 'dispiriting' it can be teaching non-gender-oriented history. She argues that history is a study of men's actions, because women were never permitted to take a seat at the table.

What is subjunctive history?

Speaking to Irwin, Dakin is flirtatious but stops short of propositioning him. They discuss the way history can change unexpectedly. Dakin's final essay explores these moments, such as Halifax going to the dentist and therefore not becoming Prime Minister.

Irwin smiles when Dakin calls it '**subjunctive** history', because he explains it using Hector's French lessons on the verb form – Dakin has **synthesised** the two teachers' educations and developed his own thinking from it.

Key Quotations to Learn

Scripps: 'Oh Poz, with your spaniel heart, it will pass.'

Hector: 'May I make a suggestion? Why can they not all just tell the truth?'
Irwin: 'It's worth trying, provided, of course, you can make it seem like you're telling the truth.'

Dakin: 'Turning points.'
Irwin: 'Oh yes. Moments when history rattles over the points.'

Dakin: 'The subjunctive is the mood you use when something might or might not have happened, when it's imagined. Hector is crazy about the subjunctive. Why are you smiling?'
Irwin: 'Nothing. Good luck.'

Summary

- The Headmaster tells Irwin to apologise to Posner's parents, who've complained.
- Dakin, Scripps and Posner discuss sex and unrequited love being educational.
- The teachers advise on presentation in mock interviews.
- Mrs Lintott tells the boys to consider a more feminist view of history.
- Dakin and Irwin discuss 'subjunctive' history.

Questions

QUICK TEST
1. What does Posner tell Scripps?
2. What does Rudge call history?
3. What does Mrs Lintott say about history?
4. Why is Irwin smiling at Dakin at the end?

EXAM PRACTICE
Using one or more of the 'Key Quotations to Learn', write a paragraph analysing how the theme of uncertainty is presented during Act 2 Part 2.

Act 2 (part 3)

You must be able to: understand the events at the end of the play.

Why is the school photograph important?

For Mrs Lintott, it captures a memory. She moves Posner to a central position and objects when Hector's excluded because the boys will want him there. The Headmaster says it's for the school, not them.

What advice does Hector give Irwin?

He says the 'tosh' – popular culture – is an antidote to make the boys less reverent and stop them holding literature at a distance. He warns Irwin about getting involved with Dakin. He tells Irwin to leave teaching, that it will lead to indifference and disillusionment.

What happens at the boys' interviews?

The boys recount their interviews to the audience from a point in the play's future. Scripps attended Eucharist services and misses the boy he used to be.

Because Irwin said he attended Corpus, Dakin goes and looks. Dakin goes to Corpus, perhaps to imagine the teacher's experience there. He also looks at a list of previous students, looking for Irwin's name.

Posner mostly stayed in his room, enjoyed the architecture and played down the Holocaust.

The teachers assume Rudge didn't get in but he was offered a place on the day. He's **self-deprecating** and says he 'did all the other stuff' they taught. One of the dons knew his father as a college servant at Christchurch. They give him a place partly to demonstrate their lack of elitism.

What happens between Irwin and Dakin?

Dakin confronts Irwin, who admits he didn't go to Oxford until he did a teaching diploma. Dakin bluntly propositions Irwin, asking him for a drink and sex.

Irwin at first declines, and tells Dakin he doesn't want to be like Hector but defends him when Dakin says he's a joke. By the end of the scene, Irwin's agreed. Dakin tells an **incredulous** Scripps that he just wanted to say thank you. He also tells him he's blackmailed the Headmaster into letting Hector keep his job.

What happens at the end?

As Scripps points out, happiness is temporary. Scripps becomes a **narrator**, pointing out the chain of events to the audience.

Hector, at the Headmaster's suggestion, takes Irwin for a ride. They crash, leaving Hector dead and Irwin in a wheelchair.

The Headmaster gives a somewhat **hypocritical**, memorial eulogy. Mrs Lintott and the boys tell the audience what happened to them, and Hector's legacy. Hector speaks directly to the boys, telling them to 'take it, feel it, and pass it on'.

Key Quotations to Learn

Posner: 'Too fucking brief. I was looking for something more ... lingering'. *The boys hoot for more so Dakin does it again.*

Scripps: 'And here history rattled over the points ...'

Headmaster: 'If I speak of Hector it is of enthusiasm shared, passion conveyed and seeds sown of future harvest. He loved language. He loved words.'

Hector: 'Pass it on boys. That's the game I wanted you to learn. Pass it on.'

Summary

- Hector warns Irwin not to stay in teaching, or to have a relationship with Dakin.
- Dakin blackmails the Headmaster over his attitude with Fiona, to keep Hector's job.
- Hector and Irwin have an accident on the motorbike; Hector dies and Irwin ends up in a wheelchair.
- There is a memorial service for Hector where Mrs Lintott tells the audience what happens to the boys in later life, and Hector addresses the audience directly.

Questions

QUICK TEST
1. What are the boys' interview experiences?
2. Why does Rudge get in?
3. Why does Hector take Irwin on the bike?
4. What happens at the memorial service?

EXAM PRACTICE
Using one or more of the 'Key Quotations to Learn', write a paragraph analysing how Bennett creates a sense of finality at the end of the play.

You must be able to: explain the significance of the way that Bennett has structured the play.

How does Bennett maintain dramatic interest?

Bennett doesn't include scene breaks, so the scenes **transition** smoothly into one another. Onstage, the actors move stage scenery and furniture as part of the action to maintain the pace of the performance. One example is the change from Irwin's television broadcast to the classroom; the word 'apotheosis' questioned by the director then defined by Posner.

Scenes also overlap – for example, when Posner tells Irwin he's homosexual and Irwin describes the scene to Mrs Lintott. These transitions maintain visual interest and create a fast-paced movement through the plot.

How does Bennett raise and lower tension?

Bennett opens each act with a **flash-forward**, first to Irwin as a government adviser and then to five years after the end of the play. Being in a wheelchair creates a **fatalistic** quality, as the audience waits for something to happen to him.

Much of the play is comic, but Bennett uses different styles of comedy to create lighter scenes, which contrast with the more serious exploration of Hector and Irwin's conflict, and of Hector's gropings.

The Headmaster's scenes often contain an element of **farce**, especially when more serious subjects are being discussed. In the French scene, he's made to appear a fool through his lack of understanding of the situation. Rudge is also a comic **counterpoint** to lighten the mood.

How does Bennett use Scripps as a narrator?

Scripps functions as a narrator, commenting directly to the audience about events onstage. These **interjections** focus the audience's attitudes, for example, when Scripps describes Irwin as a new boy, setting an expectation of Irwin and the boys' attitudes towards him.

Scripps also behaves in a **meta-theatrical** manner, drawing attention to the way the play is structured and stories are told. Towards the end of the play, he draws attention to the narrative structure of the play including the interference of the Headmaster leading to Irwin and Hector's accident, and the almost **clichéd** ending where everybody seems to be happy but then happiness can't last. These comments also create **dramatic irony** as the audience knows that something will happen and is waiting to see how the action will play out.

Mrs Lintott also sometimes narrates, including the final memorial service when she reveals the boys' futures.

Key Quotations to Learn

Scripps: 'Posner did not say it, but since he seldom took his eyes off Dakin, he knew that Irwin looked at him occasionally too ...' (Act 1.3)

Mrs Lintott: 'I have not hitherto been allotted an inner voice ...' (Act 2.1)

Scripps: 'I shouldn't have said everybody's happy, as just saying the words mean, like in a play, that the laws of **irony** were thereby activated and things began to unravel pretty quickly after that.' (Act 2.3)

Scripps: 'And here history rattled over the points ... ' (Act 2.3)

Summary

- Bennett doesn't label scene breaks. Instead, scenes blend and overlap.
- Use of flash-forwards create a fatalistic feeling, casting a shadow over the storyline.
- Comedic scenes, often with the Headmaster or Rudge, punctuate more serious scenes.
- Narration by Scripps comments on the unreal nature of theatre, as well as creating dramatic irony.

Questions

QUICK TEST
1. How do scenes change during the play?
2. How does Bennett create a lighter mood at times?
3. How does Bennett use time to change the mood?
4. What effect does Scripps' narration have?

EXAM PRACTICE
Using one or more of the 'Key Quotations to Learn', write a paragraph analysing the way Bennett creates tension during the play.

Alan Bennett's Background

You must be able to: understand how Bennett's background has affected the play's themes

Where is Alan Bennett from?

Alan Bennett was brought up in Leeds, West Yorkshire. He attended school in the 1940s and 1950s, which is earlier than the 1980s setting of the play, but he draws on his own experiences, particularly of sitting the Oxbridge exams and being tutored for them after A-Levels, a practice which has since ended.

The play is set in a grammar school in Sheffield, and the boys' experiences reflect the discomfort teenagers sometimes feel with their hometowns – they want to 'escape' and find their hometown boring. When Posner speaks to Irwin about his difficulties, *'Sheffield'* is emphasised, which suggests that the city is one of his biggest issues, as well as implying that his home city won't accept the rest of his character.

The teachers, especially Hector in Act 1, encourage the boys to have more realistic expectations than applying to Oxford and Cambridge – in the end, it is unrealistic that they would all get in. Instead, he tells them to apply to 'Derby, Leicester, Nottingham ... Sheffield' universities in the Midlands or the North, which are considered less prestigious than Oxbridge – although they are still good-quality places to study.

In Bennett's introduction to the play, he discusses going to Oxford for interview and the sense of inadequacy he experienced, for example, not fitting in because he didn't know what to wear on the way to the communal bathroom. This idea of not fitting in is reflected through Irwin's intense desire to have people think he went to Oxford, rather than Bristol, and in the boys' desire to attend no matter what they have to do to get there.

What is Alan Bennett's theatrical experience?

Bennett started writing for television and theatre in the 1960s. His characters are often from Yorkshire, down-to-earth and **pragmatic**. Bennett is often considered by critics to be excellent at capturing the tones and rhythms of Yorkshire speech and attitudes in a realistic way. Elements can be seen of this in the black humour that is used in *The History Boys*, particularly regarding Hector's paedophilic behaviour and the boys' reactions to it.

Summary

- Alan Bennett grew up in Leeds in the 1940s and 1950s.
- His experiences of living in Yorkshire and moving south, to Oxford then London, are reflected in the play's location of Sheffield.
- At Oxford, he often felt he didn't really fit in because of his background.

Questions

QUICK TEST
1. When and where did Bennett grow up?
2. What kind of characters does Bennett often write?
3. How does his sense of being from Yorkshire come across in the play's characters?

EXAM PRACTICE
In Act 1, Hector says to the boys: 'I thought all that silliness was over with. I thought that after last year we were settling for the less lustrous institutions ... Derby, Leicester, Nottingham'. Irwin later tells them 'Go to Newcastle and be happy'.

Relating your ideas to the social context, write a paragraph explaining how Bennett's background influences his ideas in the play.

You must be able to: understand the influence of different educational contexts in the play.

Which educational contexts are important?

Several contexts are useful for this play. The first is Bennett's own educational experience at school and university. Second is the 1980s setting of the play. Third, there is the 2000s, when Bennett was writing the play.

What were Bennett's educational influences?

Alan Bennett went to school in the 1940s and university in the 1950s. He attended a grammar school in Leeds, meaning he had to pass the 11-plus test (approximately 25 per cent of students went to grammars, 75 per cent to secondary moderns). In 1965, the 11-plus started to be phased out, although there are still a few grammar schools in some areas of the UK.

Bennett writes that his Headteacher developed activities more common at independent (fee-paying) schools, including pushing more students to apply for Oxbridge. Then, entrance exams took place a year after finishing A-Levels, at the colleges. Bennett, like Posner, was impressed by the architecture. However, Bennett has Hector say that had *he* gone to Oxford he never would have worked out the difference between the smell of cold stone and learning – an ironic comment, perhaps Bennett making fun of himself.

Bennett writes that he didn't have teachers like Irwin or Hector. He taught himself to revise in a 'journalistic' style, to achieve a first-class degree. Bennett struggled to feel like he fitted in, partly because of the difference in his previous experiences and background.

How do changes in the education system affect Bennett's views in the play?

Most of the changes to education that are discussed in the play were made through the 1990s and early 2000s, rather than by the 1980s in which the play is set. Writing in 2004, Bennett is looking back at several factors.

League tables, which were introduced to England in 1992, are public lists of schools ranked in order by their exam outcomes. League tables in part were designed to make schools more competitive and want to improve in order to rise up the league tables and attract more students – a marketplace, competitive approach to education. However, contrary to the Headmaster's implication, Oxbridge entrance is not reported on league tables, and the boys already have their A-Levels, so can't improve the school's ranking in any case.

Why are some of Bennett's ideas anachronistic?

Anachronistic means something belongs to a period that isn't the one being portrayed. While writing, Bennett realised the Oxbridge entrance exams had changed since his experience. He kept the storyline as 'the ordeal' of the weekend is a more dramatic concept. Bennett's use of educational changes is often not accurate but used to create a more dramatic narrative. For example, it's unlikely that a grammar school would have eight entrants for History alone – or that they would all obtain places. It is possible that Bennett has dismissed the facts, much as Irwin would, for the sake of a good story.

Summary

- Bennett draws on his own educational experiences to inform his portrayal of the boys.
- The 1980s setting of the play enables Bennett to explore the changing economics and marketplace/status of education.
- Like Posner, Bennett struggled to fit in due to having different origins to the independently educated students at university, although unlike Posner, Bennett successfully graduated.

Questions

QUICK TEST

1. Which contexts do you need to consider when writing about education in the play?
2. How did Bennett feel about being at Oxford for his interview?
3. What changes in education occurred in the 1980s and 1990s that Bennett explores in the play?
4. How are Bennett's experiences reflected in different characters' comments in the play?

EXAM PRACTICE

The Headmaster says to Mrs Lintott: 'I am thinking league tables. Open scholarships. Reports to governors'.

Relating your ideas to the social context, write a paragraph explaining how Bennett uses the Headmaster's views to explore changing attitudes in education.

Music and Song

You must be able to: understand the way that Bennett uses music and song for dramatic effect.

What are the musical allusions in the play?

Many of the music and film **allusions** are from the 1940s, representing Hector's influence. Bennett has said that one of his inspirations was hearing 'Bewitched, Bothered and Bewildered' by Ella Fitzgerald and imagining how theatrical it would be as sung by a boy with an unbroken voice. In the play, Posner sings this after telling Scripps how much he hates hearing Dakin talk about sex. Other songs include Edith Piaf (a famous French singer), Gracie Fields (a 1930s film star) and the Pet Shop Boys (a 1980s pop duo, the most contemporary song/group).

Who is involved with the music and why?

Posner often sings love songs originally sung by women, with the exception of the Pet Shop Boys, one of whom is gay and the other who has not disclosed his sexuality. Music becomes a source of conflict with Posner's parents and they ban him from singing hymns (because of his Jewish heritage), although they are 'fine with Barbra Streisand', perhaps because she is Jewish. She is also a famous gay icon, making this a more ironic reference, as it seems likely his parents don't know of his homosexuality.

Scripps plays the piano to accompany Posner and also in the scenes that the characters perform for Hector. As he plays on the sidelines rather than acting, he appears separate from the other boys.

Both Scripps and Posner are detached from the 1980s youth culture of their peers – Scripps through his intensifying Christianity and Posner through his Judaism and homosexuality. They are also detached in other ways; Posner is quiet and reserved, observing his peers (particularly Dakin), while Scripps, from the beginning of the play, is practising journalistic detachment. Their absorption of Hector's 1940s culture increases this sense of distance and pushes the two of them further into friendship.

At the end, Rudge, who hasn't been much involved in the acting or singing, sings The Pet Shop Boys' 'It's a Sin'. As the only 1980s song, it's one Hector doesn't know, symbolising the boys leaving school and their teachers behind.

How does the music contribute to the dramatic effects?

As originally performed, the music accompanied film sequences projected while scene changes took place. In the script, the piano and songs provide scene transitions. They also underline emotions, for example, Posner's songs about unrequited love.

The boys sing Gracie Fields' 'Wish Me Luck As You Wave Me Goodbye' as they leave, a song often associated with the Second World War as it became a patriotic inspiration.

At Hector's memorial, they sing 'Bye Bye Blackbird', a 1920s standard. The **juxtaposition** of cheerful songs and sad events creates an ambiguous mood, intensifying the emotion and at the same time providing humour, so avoiding sentimentality.

Summary

- Most of the musical allusions are from the 1940s or earlier, except Rudge's Pet Shop Boys.
- The music is used to cover scene changes.
- The music heightens the mood onstage, especially in Posner's songs.
- Scripps often provides piano accompaniment to scenes rather than acting in them.
- Scripps and Posner's detachment is highlighted through their involvement with the music.

Questions

QUICK TEST
1. Who is most involved with the music?
2. What does Posner sing when he speaks to Scripps about Dakin?
3. What is significant about Rudge's singing at the end?
4. What does the music suggest about Scripps and Posner?

EXAM PRACTICE
Posner sings 'Bewitched, Bothered and Bewildered', which includes the line 'Lost my heart, but what of it/He is cold I agree/He can laugh, but I love it/Although the laugh's on me'.
Write a paragraph exploring how Bennett uses music to present some of his ideas.

Theatrical Devices

You must be able to: understand some of the theatrical devices that Bennett uses to present his ideas.

How does Bennett use farce?

'Farce' is a style of comedy. It entertains using unlikely or improbable situations. It often involves mistaken identity, **absurdity** and physical humour. In the French scene, Bennett uses farce in the way the boys take on roles first in the brothel and then become soldiers and doctors. The physical comedy is crucial: the boy lying on the bed as a brothel client becomes a boy lying on a medical table in a field hospital. Bennett's stage direction 'a boy begins to moan' is heard by the audiences as both the sexual sound and the groan of pain as the boys change scene at the Headmaster's entrance.

Physical comedy allows the audience to follow the action while the boys are still *acting* the brothel scene but are *speaking* the French associated with their new scene. Comedy also comes from the Headmaster's lack of knowledge so the audience joins the 'secret classroom' pact between Hector and the boys. When Hector asks the Headmaster if he understands 'soldat blessé' (meaning 'wounded soldier'), the Headmaster replies in English, therefore, unwittingly, the Headmaster translates the instructions for the boys – who might not have understood Hector's new instruction – and also tells the audience, who might not speak French.

How does Bennett use video?

It's important to understand the play in the first production. Bennett writes that scene changes are done by the boys 'under cover of film sequences of life in the school projected on a large video screen', instead of interrupting or lowering the lights.

Some of these scenes show actions not described in the play, including Dakin with Fiona (the Headmaster's secretary) and Hector walking down the corridor after his dismissal.

There is also a 'music and video sequence' of the opening of Irwin's TV show, at the beginning of Act 2, signalling his change in career and the flash-forward.

How does Bennett use narration?

Scripps provides narration, giving a perspective from beyond the events of the play. One example occurs when Irwin arrives, and Scripps tells the audience he looked like 'the new boy'.

Bennett also uses narration as meta-theatre, drawing attention to the conventions of theatre. An example is towards the end of the play when Scripps says: 'I shouldn't have said everybody's happy, as just saying the words mean, like in a play, that the laws of irony were thereby activated'. This acknowledges the fictional narrative and the expectations we have of story structures.

Summary

- Bennett uses farce – verbal and physical humour, mistaken identity and absurd situations – during the French scene.

- This humour puts the audience in collusion with Hector and the boys, against the Headmaster, who doesn't understand the scene.

- Using video sequences keeps up the pace of the action and fills in background events, such as Dakin seducing Fiona.

- Bennett uses Scripps as a narrator to create dramatic irony as he comments on the events, from a position in the future.

- This is also meta-theatrical, drawing attention to theatre conventions.

Questions

QUICK TEST
1. What is farce?
2. How is humour created in the French scene?
3. How are video scenes used?
4. What effect does Scripps' narration have?

EXAM PRACTICE

Irwin: 'Il est commotioné, peut-être?'
The classroom falls silent at the unexpected intrusion.
Hector: 'Comment?'
Irwin: 'Commotioné. Shell-shocked.'
There is a perceptible moment.

Relating your ideas to the quotation above, explore the ways in which Bennett uses different theatrical devices to present his ideas.

You must be able to: analyse how Hector is presented in the play.

How is Hector's attitude to education presented?

Hector is charismatic and entertaining. He has evidently taught the boys English Literature thoroughly in all respects – they achieved good grades and they have a wide-ranging understanding and appreciation of literature.

He sees education as being for life, not just exams. This is possibly a naive view – the boys need qualifications after all – but he has a romanticised view of education that Mrs Lintott sees as slightly patronising, suggesting the boys should limit their aspirations to avoid unhappiness. The Headmaster has always considered Hector's teaching methods 'unpredictable and unquantifiable'. The Headmaster tells Mrs Lintott that he is relieved to have a reason to fire him that 'no one can dispute.'

He went to Sheffield University. Although he applied for Oxford he says that he confused the quality of architecture with the quality of learning.

What does Hector think about literature?

For Hector, literature is a way to understand the world and human emotions.

Encouraging the boys to learn texts 'by heart', Hector teaches them that they can find comfort in the idea that someone else has had a similar experience to them.

How does Hector exploit the boys?

The boys have a warm relationship with Hector. They're often sarcastic with him but it's affectionate banter. When he breaks down, they don't know how to respond because they're used to seeing him as a teacher.

His groping them on a motorcycle is a complex issue. An audience might find this shocking, because of the implied misuse of authority – a teacher assaulting a pupil. However, Bennett asks us to question our concept of moral certainties. He deliberately chooses boys over 18 – above the age of consent – and portrays them as willing, even seeing their role as 'indulging' Hector's behaviour, characterising it themselves as harmless. They joke that they can 'only hope' it has scarred them for life, a sarcastic statement suggesting they don't take it seriously.

Key Quotations to Learn

Hector: 'The transmission of knowledge is itself an erotic act.' (Act 1.3)

Hector: 'Un-kissed. Un-rejoicing. Un-confessed. Un-embraced. Un-spent. Un-fingermarked.' (Act 1.3)

Stage direction: [Hector] *puts out his hand, and it seems for a moment as if Posner will take it, or even that Hector may put it on Posner's knee. But the moment passes.* (Act 1.3)

Hector: '... every answer a Christmas tree hung with the appropriate gobbets. Except that they're learned by *heart*. And that is where they belong ...' (Act 1.3)

Summary

- Hector is a charismatic and knowledgeable teacher.
- He believes education is for life, not just for passing exams.
- He gropes the boys on his motorbike, although they do in some measure participate.
- He views literature as crucial in understanding people and ourselves.

Sample Analysis

Hector refers to literature as 'codes, spells, runes'. The **triadic structure** emphasises how important he thinks literature can be. Bennett uses a **semantic field** of magic, suggesting that Hector sees literature as a kind of protective enchantment the boys can use in their future lives. This contrasts with the ugly-sounding way that Irwin describes the learned quotations – 'gobbets' – which Hector repeats several times, which indicates that he is angry and dismissive of Irwin's attitude.

Questions

QUICK TEST
1. How does Hector view education?
2. What relationship does Hector have with the boys?
3. How does Mrs Lintott view Hector?
4. How does the Headmaster view Hector?
5. What happens to Hector in the end?

EXAM PRACTICE
Using one or more of the 'Key Quotations to Learn', write a paragraph analysing how Bennett presents Hector as a **tragic** character.

You must be able to: analyse how Irwin is presented in the play.

What different jobs does Irwin have?

At the beginning of the play, Irwin works for the government advising on media strategy. At the opening of Act 2, he's an on-screen historian, with a journalistic approach. Both these jobs are about interpretation and presentation, but with an increasing (over time) sense of deception that makes Irwin a less than likable character.

Irwin studied a teaching diploma at Oxford, but his original degree was at Bristol, although he lies to the boys and Headmaster, leading them to believe he did study at Oxbridge. His failure to get into Oxford at first might partly explain his cynicism. His determination to get the boys into Oxbridge might be part revenge and part experiment – to enable less privileged students to get into Oxford.

What is Irwin's relationship with Dakin?

In his first lesson, Irwin tries to connect with the boys by discussing the 'foreskins of Christ', but the boys – especially Dakin – see this as patronising, trying to connect with them as a friend rather than as a teacher.

Dakin hero-worships Irwin for teaching him a different way of thinking, telling Scripps that Irwin is all he can think about. Dakin flirts with Irwin and openly invites him for sex. At first, Irwin refuses, but Dakin persuades him to accept. The accident occurs, and they never see each other again.

How does Irwin compare with Hector?

He's young, inexperienced and incredibly exam-focussed, seeing exams as the mark of achievement. He also seems to enjoy the intellectual challenge of creating an unexpected argument.

Both teachers have a sexual interest in their pupils, although Irwin doesn't act on his – partly due to the circumstances of his accident. It appears to be Dakin who controls the relationship with Irwin; he challenges, pushes and flirts while Irwin is hesitant. This questions received ideas about exploitation: who is in the position of authority and control and who is being manipulated? Both Irwin and Hector are in some cases less powerful than their pupils.

Key Quotations to Learn

Irwin: 'History nowadays is not a matter of conviction. It's a performance. It's entertainment. And if it isn't, make it so.' (Act 1.2)

Dakin: 'Reckless; impulsive; immoral ... how come there's such a difference between the way you teach and the way you live?'
Irwin: 'Actually, it's amoral.'
Dakin: 'Is it fuck. "No need to tell the truth." That's immoral.' (Act 2.3)

Irwin: 'Taking off my glasses is the last thing I do.' (Act 2.3)

Summary

- During the play, Irwin works as a teacher, on-screen historian and government adviser.
- He advises the students to improve their performance and flair to get themselves noticed.
- He flirts with Dakin and agrees to go for a drink.
- After the accident, Irwin is wheelchair-bound, as seen at the beginning of each Act.

Sample Analysis

During a lesson, Irwin tells the boys that 'A question has a front door and a back door. Go in the back, or better still, the side'. This use of **metaphor** is typical of Irwin's journalistic style and demonstrates his belief that there are no 'right' answers or facts, only interpretation. His **declarative** statements however leave little room to argue with him.

Questions

QUICK TEST
1. What jobs does Irwin have?
2. What do these jobs have in common?
3. What happens between Irwin and Dakin?
4. What does Hector tell Irwin?

EXAM PRACTICE
'We were having a discussion as to whether you are **disingenuous** or **meretricious**'.
Using one or more of the 'Key Quotations to Learn', write a paragraph discussing which of these words most applies to Irwin.

Dakin

You must be able to: analyse how Dakin is presented in the play.

What are the audience's early impressions of Dakin?

Early on the audience sees Dakin as sarcastic, dismissive of Irwin – 'ooh sir, you devil' – when Irwin attempts to shock during his first lesson.

He could be described as sex-obsessed. The brothel scene is his idea, demonstrating that he also knows how to manipulate others, including Hector.

Dakin's conversations with Scripps often include discussion of sex, particularly his relationship with Fiona, the Headmaster's secretary. Using the **extended metaphor** of the First World War to describe their sexual affair is not a flattering way of presenting his relationship. It shows Dakin's ability to synthesise and genuinely understand his learning, but also reflects his lack of empathy.

How manipulative is Dakin?

Dakin's good looks and wit enable him to charm and manipulate those around him. He's Hector and Irwin's favourite, although Mrs Lintott sees through him.

At the end of the play, Dakin uses his relationship with Fiona to blackmail the Headmaster, accusing him of 'trying to feel up Fiona'. He also offers to take a lift home, suggesting he's retained his affection for Hector.

He lacks empathy for others, his tell-all relationship with Fiona and his careless attitude regarding Posner, as well as his comment that Hector is 'a joke', suggest his lack of consideration. He also calls Hitler a 'statesman', taking his argument of the Holocaust too far because he's more interested in playing the game than genuinely understanding the history.

What does Dakin become?

He is the boy who perhaps learns the most; he puts together the two teaching styles to describe 'subjunctive history'.

However, he also remains flawed. Although Dakin manipulates others, he discusses with Irwin the difference between 'amoral' and 'immoral'; Dakin himself seems to realise that what he does – propositioning Irwin, blackmailing the Headmaster – is immoral but gets the results he wants. At the memorial service, Mrs Lintott describes him as a lawyer telling 'highly paid fibs' because it's fun, reflecting a lack of moral certainty. He didn't go for a drink with Irwin because of the wheelchair, which would have added a degree of seriousness he was unprepared to deal with.

Key Quotations to Learn

Posner: 'What have you got to look forward to?'
Dakin: 'More of the same. You can't save it up. I like him.' (Act 2.2)

Dakin: 'It's subjunctive history.' (Act 2.2)

Dakin: 'Because I went round to look at the fucking college, that's why it matters. Because I imagined you there.' *Pause.* (Act 2.3)

Summary

- Dakin is the boys' leader: sarcastic, witty and good-looking.
- He's obsessed with sex, having a relationship with Fiona and trying to seduce Irwin.
- He lacks empathy for others.
- However, he learns to knit the two teachers' lessons together, defining subjunctive history as the combination of the two.
- Dakin becomes a tax lawyer, making money for fun by telling highly paid fibs.

Sample Analysis

At the memorial, Mrs Lintott reveals Dakin became a lawyer. His flippant declarative, 'I like money. It's fun', emphasises the character's desire to have fun and prioritise entertainment above everything else. He refers to essay-writing and history as a 'game'; he doesn't take much seriously and is often presented as shallow when it comes to people and relationships.

Questions

QUICK TEST
1. How does Dakin view Irwin?
2. How does Dakin approach sex?
3. How does Dakin respond to Posner's crush on him?
4. How does Dakin save Hector's job?

EXAM PRACTICE
Using one or more of the 'Key Quotations to Learn', write a paragraph analysing how Bennett presents Dakin's attitudes towards relationships.

You must be able to: analyse how Posner is presented in the play.

What is Posner's dramatic function?

Bennett uses Posner to change scene or set the mood. He sings old standards by female singers (e.g. 'Bewitched' by Ella Fitzgerald); these songs comment on the main action and often focus on his unrequited love for Dakin.

Posner has a comic function, playing female roles including 'Simone' the prostitute and Celia Johnson's role in *Brief Encounter*. These are both funny and sad considering Posner's homosexual struggles and his experience of unrequited love.

Posner defines complex words, **glossing** them, functioning as scene transitions (e.g. opening Act 2). He is often anxious, checking his knowledge rather than being confident in his interpretations.

How does Bennett present Posner's differences?

Posner is never chosen to ride with Hector. Hector might recognise his homosexuality or that he is more vulnerable than the other boys. Posner's homosexuality is well known; he makes no secret of his love for Dakin. Bennett uses gay stereotypes for comic effect, including Posner's parents being 'fine' with him singing Barbra Streisand but not hymns.

His Jewishness is explored in the Holocaust scene. He stands up for his own views: that it is a subject like no other. However, at interview he says he 'did play it down'. In some ways, this is a betrayal of his principles. It also suggests that he struggles to convey his own ideas, reflecting the sense of insecurity that is revealed in the memorial service.

What happens to Posner at the end of the play?

Posner can be described as a tragic character. At the opening of Act 2, a 'Man' (later revealed as Posner) confronts Irwin. 'Man' says he's in counselling having dropped out of Cambridge.

In her summary of the boys' achievements, Mrs Lintott suggests Posner is the only one who took Hector's teaching to heart but her description of his life makes him sound a sad, lonely character. Even his 'friends' online don't know his real name or gender. However, Hector's teaching doesn't seem to have been effective in providing Posner with comfort after all.

Key Quotations to Learn

Stage direction: *Posner sings a verse or two of 'Bewitched' as Scripps plays and the class filters back.* (Act 1.2)

Posner: 'Aren't you frightened it's all going to be over too soon?' (Act 2.2)

Man (Posner): 'All the effort went into getting there and then I had nothing left. I found I'd got somewhere then I found I had to go on.' (Act 2.1)

Mrs Lintott: 'He haunts the local library and keeps a scrapbook of the achievements of his one-time classmates ...' (Act 2.3)

Summary

- Posner is in love with Dakin, but seems to almost enjoy the pain of unrequited love.
- His homosexuality causes him anxiety; he discusses it with Irwin but doesn't get much support.
- Hector doesn't ever give him a lift.
- Bennett uses Posner to create scene transitions and provide incidental music which heighten the mood of the scenes.

Sample Analysis

Posner offers Irwin a list of his shortcomings: 'I'm a Jew. I'm small. I'm homosexual. And I live in Sheffield. I'm fucked'. The list of declaratives with the final **taboo language** is comic. Bennett's use of 'And' invites an actor to pause and emphasise the final disadvantage – 'Sheffield' – which comically suggests his location might be the most significant problem, contrary to the audience's expectations.

Questions

QUICK TEST
1. Who is Posner in love with?
2. In what ways is Posner different?
3. How does Bennett use Posner for dramatic transition and effect?
4. What does Mrs Lintott tell us happens to Posner after the events of the play?

EXAM PRACTICE
Using one or more of the 'Key Quotations to Learn', write a paragraph analysing the way that Posner is presented as a tragic character.

Mrs Lintott

You must be able to: analyse how Mrs Lintott is presented in the play.

How does Bennett present Mrs Lintott?

She's blunt and direct – her swearing shocks Hector by describing Dakin as 'cunt-struck' ('You like compound **adjectives**') and calling the Headmaster a 'twat'. She's aware of her standing in an all-male environment, and her nickname 'Unsurprisingly, I am Tot or Totty. Some irony there, one feels'. She knows she's not seen as sexually attractive – 'I'm what men would call a safe pair of hands'. Yet she knows more than Irwin or Hector, including Posner's love for Dakin and that Dakin is dating Fiona. She's affectionate towards Hector and the boys, trying to position them together for the final photo when the Headmaster edges Hector out. When she learns of Hector's groping she sees it as foolish and is frustrated by it, refusing to let him explain away what he did, but she is still affectionate rather than condemning him.

What is Mrs Lintott's view of education?

She teaches History, thoroughly but plainly: 'This is History, not histrionics'. The Headmaster credits the boys' A-Level success to her. She values higher education, no matter where, and went to Durham, where she had several first-time experiences: 'It's the pizza that stands out'. She does understand presentation – 'It sounds better to say "I'm keen on film" than " like films"'. She also believes that teachers have a responsibility to prepare students for the real world, but without personal **bias** interfering.

How far is Mrs Lintott a feminist character?

Bennett's portrayal could be interpreted as feminist because he uses Mrs Lintott to explore the way women have been **marginalised** in history. She's also a **foil** to Hector and Irwin, because her teaching contrasts with Irwin's showmanship and Hector's aimlessness. But she also comes across as a token female character. Her feminist speeches aren't always supported by her other actions, for example, her comments about female historians are a bit clichéd and don't chime with her teaching perspective.

Key Quotations to Learn

Mrs Lintott: 'Story-telling, so much of it, which is what men do naturally.' (Act 1.2)

Mrs Lintott: '[Hector] is trying to be the kind of teacher pupils will remember. Someone they will look back on. He impinges. Which is something one will never do.' (Act 1.3)

Mrs Lintott: 'Women so seldom get a turn for a start. Elizabeth I less remarkable for her abilities than that, unlike most of her sisters, she did get a chance to exercise them.' (Act 2.2)

Mrs Lintott: 'Hector, darling, love you as I do, that is the most colossal balls.' (Act 2.3)

Summary

- Mrs Lintott is often an observer to others' behaviours and relationships.
- She's represented as feminist, exploring women's role in history.
- She teaches plainly but thoroughly and without bias, in contrast to Irwin and Hector.

Sample Analysis

Mrs Lintott's blunt, no-nonsense approach is a refreshing contrast to Irwin's showmanship. Lockwood quotes her as saying 'this is History, not histrionics'. The pun is typical of her wry, sarcastic attitude, but also implies that she does understand the importance of a turn of phrase or an attention-catching way of saying something. She attributes her desire for plain teaching to the position of women in history: 'What is history? History is women following behind with the bucket'. Her **euphemistic** avoidance of swearing here nonetheless tells the boys, and the audience, what she thinks of masculine authority, with the same sarcastic tone.

Questions

QUICK TEST
1. What does Mrs Lintott think about women in history?
2. What is Mrs Lintott's relationship with the boys like?
3. How does Mrs Lintott teach?
4. How does Mrs Lintott react to Hector's groping?

EXAM PRACTICE
Using one or more of the 'Key Quotations to Learn', write a paragraph analysing how Bennett presents Mrs Lintott as a feminist character.

Headmaster (Felix Armstrong)

You must be able to: analyse how the Headmaster is presented in the play.

What is the Headmaster's view of education?

The Headmaster represents the changes in education in the 2000s when Bennett wrote the play: he is results-driven and recognises he's working in a competitive marketplace. His attitude towards the boys' Oxbridge entrance is less about their wellbeing and more about the reputation of the school. He lists independent (fee-paying) schools, contrasted with his own school, and wants to compete with them. Unlike many state schools, the boys' school is selective.

He values exam results, causing conflict with Hector and, occasionally, Irwin, who argues there is always a bit of luck involved in Oxbridge entry.

The Headmaster is concerned for the reputation of the school more than the wellbeing of the boys. When Hector is reported he asks Hector to retire rather than firing him, in order to avoid a scandal. His reaction to the complaint from Posner's parents is similarly concerned with the school's reputation rather than whether the subject should be taught. When Irwin teaches the Holocaust the Headmaster's main concern is ensuring there is no suggestion that this atrocity didn't happen, so that Posner's Jewish parents would not be upset.

How does the Headmaster interact with the boys?

He begins to get involved with the French lesson but is flustered when Hector corrects his pronunciation, seeing it as a loss of face and authority.

The boys see him as a joke and use his first name, showing a lack of respect.

Dakin tells Scripps the Headmaster tries to 'cop a feel' of Fiona, and uses this to blackmail him into offering Hector a reprieve.

What do the teachers think of him?

The teachers also have little respect for the Headmaster. Mrs Lintott is polite to his face but sarcastically calls him 'our fearless leader' and 'twat' to others. The French scene creates a bond between the boys and Hector, who deliberately positions them against the Headmaster as it is clear he doesn't understand what is happening.

However, when the Headmaster confronts Hector and insists that this is no time for poetry, the audience might be likely to agree with him that Hector's response is inappropriate and ill-timed. However, he quickly loses **sympathy** again with his homophobic outburst.

Key Quotations to Learn

Headmaster: 'I would call it grooming, did not that have overtones of the monkey house.' (Act 1.1)

Headmaster: 'There is inspiration, certainly, but how do I quantify that?' (Act 2.1)

Headmaster: 'For each and every one of you, his pupils, he opened a deposit account in the bank of literature and made you all shareholders in that wonderful world of words.' (Act 2.3)

Headmaster: 'It's not for the boys. It's for the school.' (Act 2.3)

Summary

- The Headmaster reflects changing education.
- He is results-driven and more concerned with the reputation of the school than the boys' welfare.
- The boys and teachers both lack respect for him.
- He is hypocritical when he asks Hector to resign, as the Headmaster sexually harasses his secretary.

Sample Analysis

When speaking with Mrs Lintott, the Headmaster says: 'Think charm. Think polish. Think Renaissance Man'. His triadic structure shows his understanding of Irwin's **rhetorical** techniques designed to persuade – each pause an opportunity for his audience to reflect on what he's saying. The use of 'charm' and 'polish' implies that presentation skills are all-important, while the final '**Renaissance man**' could be **contradictory**, considering the term is used for incredibly clever individuals who are good at a range of different disciplines.

Questions

QUICK TEST

1. What does the Headmaster value about education?
2. What does the Headmaster say about Hector's results?
3. How does the Headmaster interact with the boys?

EXAM PRACTICE

Using one or more of the 'Key Quotations to Learn', write a paragraph analysing the Headmaster's attitude to education.

Scripps and Rudge

You must be able to: analyse how Bennett presents Scripps and Rudge in the play.

How does Bennett present Scripps?

Scripps functions as a narrator of the play. He also enables Posner and Dakin to reveal thoughts and emotions through conversations with him. This detachment reflects his eventual career as a journalist. Scripps is given the final comment on Hector, an indication of his importance.

Scripps is one of the most mature characters. He doesn't joke about sex like Dakin and can offer thoughtful advice and questioning, to Posner about his unrequited love, and to Irwin in the Holocaust lesson.

Scripps discusses his religious beliefs with similar detachment. He expresses profound faith, but also thinks it is a phase that will fade with age and experience.

How does Bennett present Rudge?

Rudge is portrayed as the least 'naturally clever' of the boys. Boys and teachers patronise him and sometimes make fun of his efforts to learn. However, he is one of the most hard-working. He writes lots of notes in lessons to learn. He gets on best with Mrs Lintott, telling her **sardonically** that Irwin's teaching is 'cutting edge, miss, it really is'. He's aware of the game they're learning.

The teachers are surprised when he gets in. Rudge tells them he had 'family connections' – one of the interviewers recognised his father's name, as he was a college servant there. Rudge suggests he was accepted because he's good at sports and as a way for the college to show 'how far they'd come' in accepting students from less privileged backgrounds.

Rudge's hard work and independence makes him just as successful as the others. He ends up owning a building company and is proud of his achievements.

Key Quotations to Learn

Scripps: 'Like stamp collecting, it [his faith] seems to have gone out and I suspect even the vicar thinks I am a freak.' (Act 1.1)

Scripps: 'Love apart, it is the only education worth having.' (Act 2.3)

Rudge: 'How come they told me or how come they took a thick sod like me? I have family connections.' (Act 2.3)

Rudge: 'Like them or not, Rudge Homes are at least affordable homes for first-time buyers ... Death, it's just one more excuse to patronise. I had years of that.' (Act 2.3)

Summary

- Scripps has a journalistic detachment; he functions as a narrator.
- Scripps is a **confidant** for other characters, who tell the audience their thoughts and feelings through him.
- Rudge is very sporty, good-natured and hard-working but the least naturally clever.
- Rudge is pragmatic about his offer, accepting that his background is partly responsible.

Sample Analysis

Rudge provides comic relief through his down-to-earth statements. He tells Mrs Lintott that she has 'force-fed us the facts; now we're in the process of running around acquiring flavour'. His metaphor of battery-farmed chickens is humorous and demonstrates he fully understands the 'game' they are learning. The **verb phrase** 'running around acquiring flavour' has a sarcastic tone, demonstrating his dislike for the showing off they are encouraged to do.

Questions

QUICK TEST
1. What makes Scripps seem more mature than the other boys?
2. What is Scripps' attitude to his religious beliefs?
3. Why does Rudge get into Cambridge?
4. What is Rudge's job at the end of the play?

EXAM PRACTICE
Using one or more of the 'Key Quotations to Learn', write a paragraph analysing the way Rudge or Scripps is presented in the play.

You must be able to: analyse how Bennett uses some of the minor characters to present his ideas.

Who are the 'minor' characters in the play?

Timms, Lockwood, Akthar and Crowther aren't given as clearly defined characteristics as the other students. Of the four boys, Timms has the most developed character and often plays the class clown. In their classroom performances, he acts out comic roles, often with Lockwood, who contributes to the teasing of the teachers. Akthar has a Muslim background and sometimes comments on it alongside Posner's Judaism. Crowther in his interview says he likes acting.

The other character mentioned regularly is Fiona, although she is never seen.

What is the dramatic purpose of the other boys?

All the boys contribute to the lively, comic side of the play. They often speak in **stichomythia**, speaking consecutive lines quickly as a trio, working together to provide witty banter in response to Irwin or Hector's questioning. Their comments usually include overuse of 'sir', which makes them sound more gentle in their mocking. Their roles need good comic delivery and timing onstage to emphasise the jokes.

What is the purpose of Fiona's character?

Although she's never seen onstage (except sometimes in video clips during scene changes), Fiona plays an important role. Dakin discusses his attitude towards her and sex, using the metaphor of warfare to describe their relationship. Mrs Lintott suggests that Dakin might also know more about the workings of the school through Fiona, indicating that Mrs Lintott doesn't trust Fiona's discretion. It is later Fiona who tells Dakin that Hector has been asked to leave, although not quite all of the details about how he was discovered. According to Dakin, the Headmaster also 'chases her round the desk' and Dakin uses this information to blackmail the Headmaster into giving Hector his job back.

By referring to Fiona only in terms of her usefulness, Bennett presents her as a sex object for Dakin. More widely, her character contributes to Mrs Lintott's complaint about the lack of female voices, drawing further attention to the masculinity that dominates the play as a result of Bennett's decision to use the setting of a school for boys.

Key Quotations to Learn

Timms: 'A joke, sir. Oh. Are jokes going to be a feature, sir? We need to know as it affects our mind-set.' (Act 1.1)

Posner: 'What Fiona is presumably carrying out is a planned withdrawal. You're not forcing her. She's not being overwhelmed by superior forces ... you're just negotiating over the pace of the occupation.' (Act 1.2)

Lockwood: 'It's locked against the Forces of Progress, sir.'
Crowther: 'The spectre of Modernity.'
Akthar: 'It's locked against the future, sir.' (Act 1.2)

Summary

- The four other boys create comedy through their dialogue and timing.
- They often speak together, heightening their comic delivery.
- Fiona is never seen onstage but is used by Dakin as a way to reinstate Hector.
- Bennett's representation of Fiona suggests the insignificance of women in this environment.

Sample Analysis

Rudge: 'Fuck 'em.'
Dakin: 'Currently I am seeing Fiona,'

By juxtaposing these lines, Bennett implies that Fiona is a sexual target for Dakin, associating her with Rudge's crude language. The comedy associated with Dakin's references to Fiona, portraying her as a recreational activity, suggests that women have little significance in this male-dominated environment.

Questions

QUICK TEST
1. What are the other four boys' names and main characteristics?
2. How is Fiona's relationship with Dakin presented?
3. How does Fiona's character contribute to Mrs Lintott's arguments?

EXAM PRACTICE
Using one or more of the 'Key Quotations to Learn', write a paragraph analysing how Bennett uses one or more of the minor characters to present his ideas.

You must be able to: analyse how Bennett presents different ideas about education.

What are the main ideas about education in the play?

The conflict in the play centres on the purpose of education – whether schools are equipping students to pass exams and enter the workplace, or for a wider, life-long education.

What do different teachers think about education?

Irwin's behaviour focusses on education for qualifications and business success. He is exam-driven, focussing on the boys' presentational style rather than historical truth. However, these are important skills – the journalistic style ensures they stand out.

Hector's post-A-Level teaching focusses on cultural experience, equipping the boys to compete. In 2013, the UK Government argued that cultural capital is essential to social mobility. Hector's teaching provides this, studying literature the boys wouldn't otherwise have encountered.

Mrs Lintott's view is expressed when discussing whether Hector is a 'good' teacher. She refers to 'droves of the half-educated' being taught they could become artists. Her comment can be interpreted as dismissing artistic careers as easier and a lack of education restricting career choices to traditionally low-paying jobs. That the boys become magistrates, lawyers, headmasters and successful business owners indicates they overcome any barriers because of their education. However, given Bennett's own career as a writer, it might also be slightly sarcastic – some clearly can make a living as artists.

The Headmaster's view of education centres on the continued reputation and ambition of the school. He is more concerned with league tables and 'competing' with independent schools, rather than the boys' prospects.

What do the boys think about education?

The boys experience both alternatives – Irwin's exam-focus and Hector's wider cultural-based teaching forbidden in the exam. By the end of the play, they have brought together Hector and Irwin's educational values and passed their exams. After leaving school, they have developed an appreciation of the importance of Hector's education. Posner is the only pupil who takes Hector's teachings entirely to heart, but his final description makes an audience feel deeply sorry for him, and question whether his education has let him down considering his lack of success and happiness.

Key Quotations to Learn

Hector: 'Nothing that happens here has anything to do with getting on, but remember, open quotation marks, "All knowledge is precious whether or not it serves the slightest human use,"' (Act 1.1)

Irwin: 'Education isn't something for when they're old and grey and sitting by the fire. It's for now. The exam is next month.' (Act 1.3)

Hector: 'I count examinations ... as the enemy of education.' (Act 1.3)

Mrs Lintott: 'Hector never bothered with what he was educating these boys for.' (Act 2.3)

Summary

- Bennett explores the purpose of education in schools.
- Irwin is exam-focussed, in contrast to Hector's wider, cultural education for life.
- Mrs Lintott expresses a view suggesting education is essential for all students.
- The Headmaster is focussed on gaining good exam results and league table positions that enhance the school's reputation.
- The boys combine the purposes of Irwin and Hector, and also achieve both Mrs Lintott and the Headmaster's goals.

Sample Analysis

The Headmaster disapproves of Hector's methods: 'There is inspiration, certainly, but how do I quantify that?' His methodical verb 'quantify' reflects a social attitude that education is for qualifications and the workplace, contrasting with Hector's lifelong cultural education. It echoes the Headmaster's financial metaphor in Hector's memorial service, describing the boys' education in terms of economic successes.

Questions

QUICK TEST

1. What is Hector and Irwin's disagreement on the purpose of education?
2. What does Mrs Lintott think about education?
3. What does the Headmaster value about education?
4. How do the boys view education?

EXAM PRACTICE

Using one or more of the 'Key Quotations to Learn', write a paragraph analysing the different attitudes towards education that Bennett explores.

Teaching Styles

You must be able to: analyse how Bennett presents different approaches to teaching.

What teaching styles are there in the play?

Hector and Irwin are seen teaching onstage. Hector's close relationship with the boys shows their respect. However, there are aspects to it that challenge the audience's thinking about teacher-student relationships. Not only does he fondle them – a clear violation of his position of authority – but he hits them and throws books at them. While Hector seems to treat these incidents casually, they can be shocking.

Hector's approach is romanticised; his wide-ranging knowledge of his subject is impressive, as well as the enthusiasm he creates as the boys say they want to learn poetry by heart, at home, because Hector inspires them.

Irwin's approach is in many ways similar. Both teachers are discussion-lead – presumably also because onstage this is more dramatically entertaining. He provokes the boys to think about things critically rather than accept what they are told and to use everything they know for their purpose: passing exams.

Although we never see Mrs Lintott teaching, her style is evident through the boys' dialogue. They view her as teaching no-nonsense facts.

Which styles do the boys prefer?

Sometimes they are frustrated with Hector's apparent lack of purpose but find his lessons enjoyable. They comment they need to know what style they're receiving so they can change their response, indicating they understand different styles and can learn from them.

Dakin's synthesis – 'subjunctive history' – is the end result. They can use Hector's teaching, Mrs Lintott's facts and Irwin's presentation: all these styles are useful when put together.

What is Rudge's response to teaching?

Rudge wants to know from Irwin what to write down, suggesting this is how he's been taught. He describes Mrs Lintott's style as 'Point A. Point B.', suggesting that they were taught specific interpretations. This also demonstrates the change in expectation from A-Level to University, as Irwin teaches what he says Dons (a term for university teachers) want at interview, rather than a solid A-Level exam technique.

Key Quotations to Learn

Rudge: 'So what's the verdict then, sir? What do I write down?'
Irwin: 'You can write down, Rudge, that "I must not write down every word the teacher says."' (Act 1.2)

Irwin: '... truth is no more at issue in an examination than thirst at a wine-tasting or fashion at a striptease.' (Act 1.2)

Timms: 'It depends if you want us thoughtful. Or smart.' (Act 2.1)

Rudge: 'Firm foundations type thing. Point A. Point B. Point C. Mr Irwin is more ... free-range?' (Act 1.2)

Summary

- Hector's approach is eccentric, relying on his relationship with the boys.
- Hector's style requires the boys to absorb information, which they're not all equally successful at doing.
- Irwin's style relies on presentation skills, practising essay writing to create unusual arguments.
- Mrs Lintott isn't seen onstage teaching but is described as logical, factual and thorough.
- The synthesis of these styles leads to the boys' success.

Sample Analysis

As he returns essays, Irwin's repetition 'Dull ... dull ... abysmally dull', reflects his journalistic leanings, wanting more flair in the boys' essays than truth, but his blunt honesty is similar to Hector and Lintott's pragmatic, open approaches. His hyperbolic 'abysmally' is more abrasive than might be expected and also demonstrates his challenging attitude.

Questions

QUICK TEST
1. What is the main difference between Irwin and Hector's styles?
2. How does Rudge have difficulty with these styles?
3. What do we know about Mrs Lintott's teaching?

EXAM PRACTICE
Using one or more of the 'Key Quotations to Learn', write a paragraph analysing the ways Bennett presents the theme of teaching.

The Importance of Literature

You must be able to: analyse how Bennett presents literature.

What dramatic effect do the literary allusions have?

Bennett's play has many literary allusions. Some are attributed, such as *Drummer Hodge* by Thomas Hardy, while some are quoted without the audience necessarily knowing the author.

Literary quotations highlight the emotion that is happening onstage – Posner's recitation of *Drummer Hodge* echoes the loneliness of Hector, cast adrift after his dismissal. Quotations are used to discuss the play's themes, such as the Wittgenstein quotation when discussing the Holocaust.

What are the different views of literature?

Bennett presents the characters as loving literature. They are all interested in literature and see reading widely as essential, for different reasons.

Hector instills a love of learning and literature in the boys but not a reverence, suggesting he believes everybody should have a wider cultural knowledge and that this isn't reserved for the wealthy or privileged. Although Hector says he wants the boys to be able to compete, Mrs Lintott sees his teaching as aimless – which is not the same as pointless.

The boys see literature as joy (Scripps), consolation (Dakin) and baffling (Timms). At the memorial service, Hector tells the boys to 'take it, feel it, and pass it on' – literature is used to convey emotion.

What are some of the allusions in the play?

There are some patterns in the allusions Bennett has chosen to feature in the play.

Auden and Housman were both poets and in the play their homosexuality is alluded to, suggesting a sympathy between them and Hector.

The literature Hector most frequently teaches are classics – including Shakespeare and Housman – widely acknowledged as having outstanding or enduring characteristics. He also teaches some poets relatively contemporary to the semi-1980s setting, including Auden, Larkin and Stevie Smith (the only female writer alluded to).

Most of the allusions are pre-1970, reflecting Hector's education, as well as Bennett's – perhaps suggesting that classic literature needs to have withstood some time before it can be truly appreciated.

Key Quotations to Learn

Timms: 'Most of the stuff poetry's about hasn't happened to us yet.' (Act 1.2)

Posner: 'Literature is medicine, wisdom, elastoplast. Everything. It isn't, though, is it, sir?' (Act 1.3)

Dakin: 'All literature is consolation ... it's written when the joy is over. Finished. So even when it's joy, it's grief. It's consolation.' (Act 1.3)

Hector: 'The best moments in reading are when you come across something – a thought, a feeling, a way of looking at things – which you had thought special and particular to you. Now here it is, set down by someone else, a person you have never met, someone even who is long dead. And it is as if a hand has come out and taken yours.' (Act 1.3)

Summary

- Literary allusions intensify the emotion of a scene.
- Literature is used to explore relationships, for example, *Drummer Hodge*.
- Literature is used to understand wider themes.
- Literature is described as joy and consolation.
- Hector teaches that literature is designed to capture and express emotion.

Sample Analysis

Hector tells Irwin he didn't want the boys to talk about words 'in that reverential way that is somehow Welsh'. This description comically suggests a way of speaking that many will identify, a 'poetry voice'. The adjective 'reverential' has a tone of dismissal or rejection, as Bennett is suggesting that literature should be a part of the everyday rather than removed from it and treated differently. However, Hector also recognises the difference between 'tosh', a **colloquial** phrase of his era meaning nonsense, and 'literature'; the different **nouns** suggest that some culture has less value than others.

Questions

QUICK TEST
1. What are the dramatic effects of the literary allusions?
2. What is one significance of the Auden and Housman quotations?
3. Why does Hector teach music and film as well?
4. How do the boys view literature?

EXAM PRACTICE
Using one or more of the 'Key Quotations to Learn', write a paragraph analysing the way Bennett explores the importance of literature.

The Importance of History

You must be able to: analyse how Bennett presents the importance of history.

What are the different attitudes to history in the play?

The main conflict over history in the play is over how to interpret and present it.

In Act 1, Irwin discusses the First World War. He argues that, contrary to the list of factors the boys recite, Britain was just as culpable for the start of the war, and its severity, but doesn't acknowledge it because of the cost to its own people. Here, Irwin identifies the multi-faceted nature of history and that the victors write the history books.

Scripps, as narrator, comments 'history rattled over the points', a reminder to the audience that people like to construct history as an understandable narrative.

How does Irwin think of history?

Irwin's interpretations of history are often called journalistic, foreshadowing his future careers as TV historian and government media strategist. He argues there is 'no period so remote as the recent past' because people lack the detachment to be able to see it clearly, comparing interpretations of the dissolution of the monasteries and the Holocaust.

Irwin suggests that 'truth' is flexible, open to interpretation. This argument removes the idea of facts; everything is seen through an angle or bias.

How does Mrs Lintott think of history?

Rudge describes Mrs Lintott as teaching 'Point A. Point B.', and their listing of factors contributing to the First World War demonstrate a thorough understanding of the conventional interpretation.

She is aware of bias in interpretations, such as discussing her feminist attitude with Hector and Irwin. However, she makes clear that she has avoided imposing this view on the boys' education.

Key Quotations to Learn

Mrs Lintott: 'Men are [clever], at history, of course.'
Hector: 'Why history particularly?'
Mrs Lintott: 'Story-telling so much of it, which is what men do naturally.' (Act 1.2)

Mrs Lintott: 'History's not such a frolic for women as it is for men. Why should it be? They never get round the conference table ... History is a commentary on the various and continuing incapabilities of men. What is history? History is women following behind with the bucket.' (Act 2.2)

Irwin: 'We still don't like to admit the war was even partly our fault because so many of our people died. A photograph on every mantelpiece.' (Act 1.2)

Summary

- Mrs Lintott teaches History based on plain-speaking facts.
- Irwin argues for a more journalistic style, focussing on the influence of a strong argument.
- Irwin's approach recognises the different possible interpretations of history, depending on perspective.
- Bennett uses Scripps to remind us that people like to see history as an understandable, logical narrative.

Sample Analysis

Rudge says twice: 'History's just one fucking thing after another', and this can be comically entertaining for an audience. Because Rudge is frequently presented as less intelligent, it can seem as though he doesn't understand the complexities of history. However, as the play concludes, this statement comes to reflect the unchangeable nature of history – it always progresses – and the way that we try to impose a narrative structure on it, to help us understand it.

Questions

QUICK TEST
1. How does Irwin's attitude to history foreshadow his future careers?
2. How does Mrs Lintott teach history?
3. What does Scripps, as narrator, suggest, and how does this contrast with Rudge's view?
4. What does Irwin's teaching about the First World War suggest?

EXAM PRACTICE
Using one or more of the 'Key Quotations to Learn', write a paragraph analysing how Bennett presents interpretations of history.

You must be able to: analyse how Bennett explores ideas about the nature of truth.

What is truth?

'Truth' can be understood as the quality of being real, factual and honest.
In *The History Boys*, truth is often linked with the interpretation of history and discussions about the presentation of history.

Which characters can be considered truthful?

The most truthful characters might be the most straightforward. Rudge, for example, is plain-spoken and blunt. He values the facts, learns by writing things down and acknowledges that there is 'no barring accidents': things happen as they happen, not as you wish they would happen.

Scripps is often a character of truth, commenting as a narrator outside the storyline, but also guiding the audience's impressions of the drama. Mrs Lintott's teaching could be considered the most truthful as she attempts to teach a non-gender-biased version of history.

How does Irwin influence the interpretation of truth?

Irwin openly dismisses the possibility of teaching 'truth' in history, acknowledging that everyone has a subjective interpretation of events. He frequently tells the boys that the concept of truth is irrelevant, and the ability to persuade is more important – this will change perceptions of truth.

However, while discussing the Holocaust, Irwin cautions Dakin that to put the Holocaust in the context of foreign policy is 'inexpedient': Dakin has gone too far and risks sounding dismissive. The discussion in the play seems to suggest that the Holocaust should be taught as Hector wants, with a response guided by emotion – but this is contrary to the teaching of other historical events.

What does Hector think?

Hector advises the boys to tell the truth in their Oxbridge interviews and challenges Irwin on his interpretation of the Holocaust as having an angle.

However, Hector's own actions are often untruthful or dishonest: he tells the Headmaster 'nothing happened' on the motorbike and tries to explain himself to Mrs Lintott by saying that it was a 'laying on of hands', denying responsibility for his actions.

Key Quotations to Learn

Irwin: 'Truth is no more at issue in an examination than thirst at a wine-tasting or fashion at a striptease.' (Act 1.2)

Dakin: '"No need to tell the truth?" That's immoral.' (Act 2.3)

Hector: 'Why can they not all just tell the truth?' (Act 2.2)

Scripps: 'I thought that we'd already decided that ... truth is, if not an irrelevance, then so relative as just to amount to another point of view.' (Act 2.1)

Summary

- Rudge exemplifies truth, as he is plain-spoken, deliberate and recognises that there is no control over history.
- Scripps sometimes functions as a truth-teller through his narration, but he also guides the audience's interpretations.
- Mrs Lintott has taught plain facts, on a non-gender-oriented basis.
- Hector speaks in favour of truth but his actions sometimes suggest the opposite, particularly related to his personal behaviour.

Sample Analysis

Irwin's first speech in the play advises the deliberate hiding of truth: 'paradox works well and mists up the windows'. His metaphor suggests that trying to make truth unrecognisable or difficult to see is more likely to lead to agreement. He continues, 'the loss of liberty is the price we pay for freedom', exemplifying the paradox, and using the alliteration 'loss/liberty', 'price/pay' to heighten the **emotive** impact of his statement.

Questions

QUICK TEST
1. How do Dakin and Irwin conflict over truth regarding the Holocaust?
2. How does Irwin view truth?
3. How does Hector view truth?
4. What is Mrs Lintott's attitude to teaching history?

EXAM PRACTICE
Using one or more of the 'Key Quotations to Learn', write a paragraph analysing the way Bennett presents ideas about truth.

Sexuality

You must be able to: analyse how Bennett presents the theme of sexuality.

How is sex discussed?

Much of the discussion of sex in the play is problematic; sex is treated dismissively as merely fun divorced from relationships (Scripps, Rudge), associated with violence (Dakin's metaphors for Fiona), manipulative (Dakin with Irwin, the Headmaster's attempted groping of Fiona) or as something furtive, disappointing (Mrs Lintott, the Headmaster) or exploitative.

How does Bennett present heterosexuality?

Dakin uses the extended metaphor of the First World War to describe his seduction of Fiona, creating violent and disturbing associations. Rudge is more pragmatic and doesn't discuss sex much, his is perhaps a more mature response yet he still views sex as merely another recreational activity.

Mrs Lintott dismissively alludes to sex in her 'other things' remark, as it didn't 'stand out'. The Headmaster's pleasure in removing Hector results in his wife being the subject of 'unaccustomed sexual interference', a grotesquely comic image. This, and his attempts to 'feel up' Fiona, suggest that women have less sexual power and control than men.

Heterosexuality is also fluid – almost a 'starting point'. Posner realises during the play that he is homosexual and there are several other characters who express homosexual or bisexual desires.

What are the attitudes to homosexuality in the play?

Several characters express homophobic views, **congruent** with the 1980s setting of the play. This was a time of increasing openness about homosexuality and gay culture but the prevalence of HIV and AIDS (discovered in 1983) scared people. These diseases were sometimes called the gay plague, because the first community to fall ill from HIV (which became AIDS) was the gay community. This fear led to further prejudice against homosexuals.

The Headmaster is the most obviously homophobic character in his swearing rant towards Hector, but there are frequent slurs and derogatory language is used. However, there is also great affection for homosexual characters – Scripps for Posner, for example.

Is Hector a paedophile?

Bennett has previously written 'I think I've been criticised for not taking this seriously enough. I'm afraid I don't take that very seriously if they're 17 or 18. I think they are actually much wiser than Hector. Hector is the child, not them'. Current increased vigilance perhaps means that today's audience is more unwilling to accept any abuse of power than Bennett's contemporary 2004 audience – and Hector is, after all, the boys' teacher. It is unclear how long this behaviour has been going on, but it seems established by the beginning of the play.

Key Quotations to Learn

Timms: 'Wasn't he a nancy, sir?' (Act 1.1)

Dakin: 'Are we scarred for life, do you think?'
Scripps: 'We must hope so.' (Act 2.1)

Posner: 'Some of the literature says it will pass.'
Irwin: 'I wanted to say "the literature" might say it does but that literature doesn't.' (Act 1.3)

Mrs Lintott: 'Hector, darling, love you as I do, that is the most colossal balls.'
Hector: 'Is it?'
Mrs Lintott: 'A grope is a grope. It is not the Annunciation. You ... twerp.' (Act 2.3)

Summary

- There are no positive representations of sex in the play.
- Posner, Dakin, Irwin and Hector all express homosexual desire in diverse ways.
- There are several homophobic attitudes expressed, including from the Headmaster, and in casual insults from the boys.
- Hector's groping is an abuse of power but Bennett maintains Hector is not a paedophile.

Sample Analysis

While confronting Hector, the Headmaster bursts out violently: 'Fuck the Renaissance. And fuck literature and Plato and Michelangelo and Oscar Wilde and all the other shrunken violets you people line up'. This taboo language, entirely inappropriate to the situation, might be shocking to an audience. The Headmaster's list of gay cultural figures also indicates his homophobia, along with the derogatory 'shrunken violets' and 'you people', classifying all gay people as the same: degenerate.

Questions

QUICK TEST
1. Who expresses homosexual desires?
2. How do Dakin and Rudge's attitudes to sex differ?
3. What is Mrs Lintott's reference to sex and what does it imply?
4. What is Scripps' attitude to homosexuality?
5. What does Bennett say about Hector's groping of the boys?

EXAM PRACTICE
Using one or more of the 'Key Quotations to Learn', write a paragraph analysing the different attitudes to sexuality in the play.

Hope and Failure

You must be able to: analyse how Bennett explores ideas about hope and failure.

How is the theme of education linked with hope?

The ambition of the boys aiming for Oxbridge is hopeful and optimistic (although unrealistic, in the context of a single state school). They are all successful, and all – except Posner – go on to have prestigious, traditionally successful careers.

Does Hector's teaching reflect hope or failure?

Hector tells the boys he's creating an 'antidote' for grief, love, happiness – any emotions.

Mrs Lintott criticises Hector for not considering what he was educating the boys for. Educational theories often discuss which texts are essential to create a cultural knowledge; Irwin reflects this when he describes the students who go to Rome and study what they see there, but the Headmaster calls Hector's version of culture 'cock-eyed'. All these different perspectives, however, suggest that in order for all students to have equality of opportunity, they must be offered a cultural education, which Hector does. While not necessarily useful for a workplace, this cultural education enables them to begin to participate on the same level as the independent school candidates they are competing against.

How does Posner represent hope or failure?

At the opening of Act 2, we learn that Posner has left university, having had a nervous breakdown, and is trying to start a career in journalism (he's written an article about Irwin, but the newspaper won't publish without a quote). He is in therapy, and Mrs Lintott's speech at the end of the play reveals his life. Living alone, with only online friends who don't know his true identity, he conveys a sense of unfulfilled potential and lack of direction.

In an interview, Bennett described Posner as the 'saddest' character because he is the most unfulfilled at the end.

Key Quotations to Learn

Mrs Lintott: '... there was a consoling myth that not very bright children could always become artists. Droves of the half-educated left school with the notion that art or some form of self-realisation was a viable option.' (Act 2.1)

Hector: 'It brings a sense of not sharing, of being out of it ... a holding back. Not being in the swim.' (Act 1.3)

Mrs Lintott: 'He has long since stopped asking himself where it went wrong.' (Act 2.3)

Hector: 'Take it, feel it, and pass it on. Not for me, not for you, but for someone, somewhere, one day. Pass it on, boys.' (Act 2.3)

Summary

- Education can provide hope – of achievement and success – or failure, to do well or to live up to potential.
- Hector teaches the boys hope, to expect the best and to feel part of humanity, rather than being alone.
- Mrs Lintott criticises Hector's lack of focus on the boys' attainment, seeing education as essential for all students to have equality of opportunity.
- Bennett described Posner as the saddest character because he has the most unfulfilled potential.
- The other boys succeed in terms of their careers and personal prosperity.

Sample Analysis

Mrs Lintott's statement at the memorial describes the boys as 'pillars of a community that no longer has much use for pillars'. While her idiom describes the boys optimistically – pillars are strong, supportive, essential, her second **clause** undercuts their achievements as they are not useful after all, so have become irrelevant.

Questions

QUICK TEST
1. How does Hector's teaching prepare the boys for hope?
2. How does Hector's teaching fail the boys?
3. Is Posner a failure?
4. How does Bennett link educational success with hope?

EXAM PRACTICE
Using one or more of the 'Key Quotations to Learn', write a paragraph analysing the way Bennett presents the theme of hope and failure.

Social Privilege

You must be able to: analyse how Bennett explores social privilege in the play.

What is social privilege?

The idea of 'privilege' is that certain rights, cultural attitudes, abilities or experiences are only available to some social groups. In the play, Bennett's characters discuss expectations of the students based in part on their backgrounds rather than their abilities.

Where do Bennett's characters fit in?

Bennett explores the expectations of people from different backgrounds. The teachers are university graduates. They attended Hull (Headmaster), Bristol (Irwin), Sheffield (Hector) and Durham (Mrs Lintott), arguably the most prestigious university of the four. The boys have excellent educational achievement in their A-Level grades, but are still encouraged to reduce their expectations and ambition – to 'settle' for other universities. Rudge is especially looked down on as lacking the flair needed for Oxford. When he's offered a place, it's because his father was a college servant, implying that he's being used to fill a quota so Oxford can show its improved record of social equality. However, he becomes one of the most successful of the boys.

How does Irwin explain social divisions?

When teaching the boys polish, Irwin tells them that at the 'time of the Reformation there were fourteen foreskins of Christ preserved', a shock tactic to explain that they are competing against students who have travelled, are cultured and well-educated, as well as being trained to pass these exams. His implication is that other applicants will be from private schools and wealthy backgrounds, in comparison to the boys in front of him, who are from less priviliged backgrounds. He tells them instead 'Go to Newcastle and be happy'.

How does the play's ending contribute to this theme?

The boys, except Posner, do extremely well – this is largely attributed to their education. They have professional, relatively wealthy occupations, working as magistrates, a headmaster, the owner of a chain of dry-cleaners, and a tax lawyer. Rudge becomes proud owner of 'Rudge Homes', building 'affordable homes for first-time buyers'. They are all commended for being 'pillars of the community'.

Key Quotations to Learn

Irwin: '... they will have been to Rome and Venice, Florence and Perugia and they will doubtless have done courses on what they have seen there.' (Act 1.1)

Irwin: 'Hate them because these boys and girls against whom you are to compete have been groomed like thoroughbreds for this one particular race.' (Act 2.1)

Rudge: 'College servant's son, now an undergraduate, evidence of how far they had come, wheel come full circle and all that.' (Act 2.3)

Summary

- Irwin contrasts the boys with more culturally educated students, who are taught differently and know how to pass the entrance exams.
- The boys are encouraged to settle for less ambitious goals.
- The boys (except perhaps Posner) all become successful in different ways.

Sample Analysis

Irwin tells the boys to 'go to Newcastle and be happy'. His **imperative** sounds slightly dismissive, portraying Newcastle as a lesser option, yet it also acknowledges that Oxbridge, with its associated academic pressures, is not a suitable option for everybody. It suggests that happiness is a far more important life goal, and foreshadows Posner's difficulties as he gets into Cambridge but then realises he didn't know what to do once he was there.

Questions

QUICK TEST
1. What is Bennett's attitude towards different universities?
2. How does the boys' experience reflect their backgrounds?
3. What is Irwin's opinion of the different experiences other students will have?

EXAM PRACTICE
Using one or more of the 'Key Quotations to Learn', write a paragraph analysing the way that Bennet explores attitudes to social privilege in the play.

Tips and Assessment Objectives

You must be able to: understand how to approach the exam question and meet the requirements of the mark scheme.

Quick Tips

- You will get a choice of two questions. Do the one that best matches your knowledge, the quotations you have learned and the things you have revised.

- Make sure you know what the question is asking you. Underline key words and pay particular attention to the bullet point prompts that come with the question.

- You should spend about 45 minutes on your response. Allow yourself five minutes to plan your answer so there is some structure to your essay.

- All your paragraphs should contain a clear idea, a relevant reference to the play (ideally a quotation) and analysis of how Bennett conveys this idea. Whenever possible, you should link your comments to the play's context.

- It can sometimes help, after each paragraph, to quickly re-read the question to keep yourself focussed on the exam task.

- Keep your writing concise. If you waste time 'waffling' you won't be able to include the full range of analysis and understanding that the mark scheme requires.

- It is a good idea to remember what the mark scheme is asking of you ...

AO1: Understand and respond to the play (12 marks)

This is all about coming up with a range of points that match the question, supporting you ideas with references from the play and writing your essay in a mature, academic style.

Lower	Middle	Upper
The essay has some good ideas that are mostly relevant. Some quotations and references are used to support the ideas.	A clear essay that always focusses on the exam question. Quotations and references support ideas effectively. The response refers to different points in the play.	A convincing, well-structured essay that answers the question fully. Quotations and references are well-chosen and integrated into sentences. The response covers the whole play (not everything, but ideas from both acts rather than just focussing on one or two sections).

AO2: Analyse effects of Bennett's language, form and structure (12 marks)

You need to comment on how specific words, language techniques, sentence structures, stage directions or the narrative structure allow Bennett to get his ideas across to the audience. This could simply be something about a character or a larger idea he is exploring through the play. To achieve this, you will need to have learned good quotations to analyse.

Lower	Middle	Upper
Identification of some different methods used by Bennett to convey meaning. Some subject terminology.	Explanation of Bennett's different methods. Clear understanding of the effects of these methods. Accurate use of subject terminology.	Analysis of the full range of Bennett's methods. Thorough exploration of the effects of these methods. Accurate range of subject terminology.

AO3: Understand the relationship between the play and its contexts (6 marks)

For this part of the mark scheme, you need to show your understanding of how the characters or Bennett's ideas relate to when he was writing or when the play was set.

Lower	Middle	Upper
Some awareness of how ideas in the play link to its context.	References to relevant aspects of context show a clear understanding.	Exploration is linked to specific aspects of the play's contexts to show detailed understanding.

AO4: Written accuracy (4 marks)

You need to use accurate vocabulary, expression, punctuation and spelling. Although it's only four marks, this could make the difference between a lower or a higher grade.

Lower	Middle	Upper
Reasonable level of accuracy. Errors do not get in the way of the essay making sense.	Good level of accuracy. Vocabulary and sentences help to keep ideas clear.	Consistent high level of accuracy. Vocabulary and sentences are used to make ideas clear and precise.

1. 'Hector is the best teacher in *The History Boys*'. Explore how far you agree with this statement.

   Write about:
   - how Bennett presents Hector and others' attitudes towards him
   - how Bennett uses the character of Hector to explore some of his ideas about teachers.

2. How does Bennett use Mrs Lintott to explore ideas about the importance of history?

   Write about:
   - how Bennett presents Mrs Lintott and others' attitudes towards her
   - how Bennett uses the character of Mrs Lintott to explore some of his ideas about history.

3. How does Bennett use the character of Posner to explore ideas about being different?

   Write about:
   - how Bennett presents Posner
   - how Bennett uses the character of Posner to explore some of his ideas.

4. 'Dakin's relationships are shallow and meaningless'. Explore how far you agree with this statement.

   Write about:
   - how Bennett presents the character of Dakin
   - how Bennett uses the character of Dakin to explore some of his ideas.

5. Do you think Scripps is an important character in *The History Boys*?

   Write about:
   - how Bennett presents the character of Scripps
   - how Bennett uses Scripps to explore some of his ideas.

6. 'The Headmaster is presented as the most practical of the characters in *The History Boys*'. Explore how far you agree with this statement.

   Write about:
   - how Bennett presents the character of the Headmaster
   - how Bennett uses the Headmaster to explore some of his ideas.

7. Who do you think is the best teacher in *The History Boys*?

   Write about:
   - how Bennett presents your chosen character
   - how Bennett uses your chosen character to explore some of his ideas.

8. How does Bennett present attitudes towards different types of education in *The History Boys*?

   Write about:
   - what some of the different attitudes to education are
   - how Bennett presents these attitudes in the play.

9. In *The History Boys*, Mrs Lintott says 'History is women following behind with the bucket'.

Write about:
- how Bennett presents ideas about women in the play
- how Bennett uses the character of Mrs Lintott to explore some of his ideas about women.

0. How does Bennett explore ideas about sex and sexuality in *The History Boys*?

Write about:
- what some of the different attitudes to sex and sexuality are
- how Bennett presents these attitudes in the play through the ways that he writes.

1. How does Bennett explore social privilege in *The History Boys*?

Write about:
- the ideas about social privilege in *The History Boys*
- how Bennett presents these ideas by the ways he writes.

2. *The History Boys* has been called a 'play about hope, and failure'. To what extent do you agree with this view?

Write about:
- how Bennett presents ideas about hope and failure
- how Bennett presents these ideas by the ways he writes.

3. Posner says that 'Literature is medicine, wisdom, elastoplast. Everything. It isn't though, is it?'

   How does Bennett present ideas about literature in the play?

Write about
- what some of the different attitudes to literature are
- how Bennett presents these attitudes in the play.

14. How does Bennett present ideas about missed opportunities in *The History Boys*?

Write about:
- what some of the missed opportunities are
- how Bennett presents these ideas in the play.

15. How does Bennett present characters coming into conflict in *The History Boys*?

Write about:
- why some of the characters come into conflict
- how Bennett presents these conflicts in the play.

16. Are Hector and Irwin 'good' teachers?

Write about:
- how Bennett presents Hector and Irwin as teachers
- how Bennett uses Hector and Irwin to explore some of his ideas about education.

17. What do you think is the importance of the opening of *The History Boys*?

Write about:
- how the opening of the play presents some important ideas
- how Bennett presents these ideas in the play.

18. What do you think is the importance of the ending of *The History Boys*?

Write about:
- how the ending of the play presents some important ideas
- how Bennett presents these ideas in the play.

Planning a Character Question Response

You must be able to: understand what an exam question is asking you and prepare your response.

How might an exam question on character be phrased?

It will usually look like this:

How does Bennett use the character of Hector to explore ideas about education?

Write about:

- how Bennett presents the character of Hector
- how Bennett uses Hector to explore some of his ideas.

[30 marks + 4 AO4 marks]

How do I work out what to do?

Work out the focus of the question. In this case, it is about Hector but there is further guidance to think about his impact on the educational ideas in the play. In answering character questions, it is useful to think 'What wider ideas are they being used to explore? Why are they significant and what happens to make them so?' and address the question that way.

'How' and 'why' are important elements. For AO1, you need to show understanding of the way that Hector teaches, and what other characters think about his methods.

For AO2, the word 'how' means you need to analyse the way that Bennett's use of language, structure and the dramatic form contribute to the audience's understanding of Hector, and how he's used to explore different ideas of education. Ideally you should have quoted evidence, but you can make clear reference to specific parts of the play if necessary.

You also need to remember to link your answer to context to achieve AO3 marks and write accurately to gain the four AO4 marks for spelling, punctuation and grammar.

How do I plan my essay?

You have approximately 45 minutes to answer this question.

Although it doesn't seem long, spending the first five minutes writing a quick plan helps to focus your thoughts and produce a well-structured essay, an essential part of AO1.

Try to think of five or six ideas. Each of these can become a paragraph.

You can plan however you find most useful: a list, spider diagram or flow chart. Once you have your ideas, take a moment to check which order you want to write them in.

Look at the example of a spider diagram on the opposite page.

The seeming useless nature of Hector's education ('wider reading') and the way the boys claim they don't understand it at the time 'We're making your deathbeds' (Act 1.2)
(Context: Bennett's experiences)

Conflict with Irwin; Hector's death (structure) suggests his old-fashioned style has to go. But Dakin's synthesis – 'subjunctive history' – seems to be the intellectual endgame of the play

Presentation of Hector

The fond relationship he has with the boys – stagecraft of his entrance (taking off the motorcycle leathers) as mark of respect. His 'secret pact' with them during the comedic French scene
(Stagecraft: farce/physical comedy)

Hector's fondling of the boys undermines his credibility – as he knows in his conversation with Irwin at the end. Hector's enthusiasm is more appealing than Irwin's exam focus

Literature is for life, not exams: 'Literature is medicine, wisdom, elastoplast. Everything'/'Literature is consolation' (Act 1.3) – BUT conflict: Posner disagrees and Dakin calls him a joke. Lintott – Hector's preparing boys for failure, not success
(Context: state of education)

Summary

- Make sure you understand the focus of the question (AO1).
- Analyse the way the writer conveys ideas through use of language, structure and form (AO2).
- Link ideas to social and historical context (AO3).
- Spell accurately, and use ambitious, precise vocabulary (AO4).

Questions

QUICK TEST
1. What key skills do you need to include in your answer?
2. What timings should you use?
3. Why is planning important?

EXAM PRACTICE
Plan a response to the following exam question:
How does Bennett use the character of Irwin to explore ideas about education?
Write about:
- how Bennett presents the character of Irwin
- how Bennett uses Irwin to explore some of his ideas.
[30 marks + 4 AO4 marks]

Grade 5 Annotated Response

How does Bennett use the character of Hector to explore ideas about education?

Write about:

- how Bennett presents the character of Hector
- how Bennett uses Hector to explore some of his ideas.

[30 marks + 4 AO4 marks]

At the opening of the play, Hector and the boys have a close relationship. Hector tells them that he trusts them. 'I am in your hands' (1). This closeness might be frowned on by a modern audience who see teachers as needing to be more professional and separate from their students, especially after recent scandals (2). Hector's character is used to explore different ideas about what kind of education works best. The relationship is also shown through the way Hector 'gropes' the boys and they don't report him (3). It is also clear in the French scene where the boys pretend to be doing something else so Hector doesn't get in trouble when the Headmaster walks in (4).

Alan Bennett uses the difference between Hector and Irwin to explore different answers to the question – what is education for? (5). Hector says the boys have learned their quotes 'by heart', which makes them more for wider life rather than just exams. In comparison, Irwin calls the quotes 'gobbets', which is an unpleasant noun suggesting that the quotes aren't very useful or important (6) but he says they can be used for a more interesting argument. Mrs Lintott also disagrees with Hector's methods as she doesn't think he is a good teacher (7), which makes the audience wonder whose side Bennett is on, and whose side they should be on (8).

*Bennett uses Hector's character to show that education, and learning, can be comforting. He says that reading is good when 'a hand has come out and taken yours'. This **simile** suggests that reading is comforting. It contrasts with the stage direction where Hector doesn't touch Posner, which shows that Bennett is saying learning literature isn't always what Hector thinks it is (9). Posner uses a **triadic structure** to describe Hector's attitude to literature when he says 'Literature is medicine, wisdom, elastoplast. Everything'. Although this sounds like literature is helpful, it also might mean that literature gets less useful because 'elastoplast' is less than 'medicine' (10). Hector doesn't seem to really care about exams, but they are all Irwin cares about. Mrs Lintott is in the middle, as she teaches the boys well but 'plainly', suggesting that she teaches them how to interpret the information she gives them.*

Although the audience might like the way Hector approaches education, Alan Bennett suggests that he is too old-fashioned and his groping the boys makes him an untrustworthy character (11). The Headmaster also tells the audience that Hector isn't a good teacher because he doesn't like the way he gets results and calls them 'unquantifiable'. This links with the introduction of league tables and school competition in the 1990s, although after Bennett has set the play in the 1980s (12). The Headmaster likes results, which Irwin focusses on and Hector despises. The audience finds it difficult to choose between Hector and Irwin because they both have some positive ideas about education, and they are both needed to get the boys into Oxford and Cambridge. Dakin calls the combination of the two ways of teaching 'subjunctive history' and the way Irwin reacts shows that he is proud of Dakin for putting the ideas together (13). Although Hector is old-fashioned and his death could be interpreted as Bennett saying that there isn't a place for his kind of teaching anymore, like the Headmaster, the sadness about his death and the memorial service suggest that he is well thought of and what he teaches for is important (14).

1. Quotation used, but a more useful quote could be chosen with more to explore. AO2
2. Brief reference to context. AO3
3. Explanation of character could be strengthened by more insightful exploration of the meaning of the relationship. AO1
4. Useful linking reference, but the stagecraft could be explored in more detail. AO2
5. Clear identification of attitudes to education, presented through character. AO1/AO2
6. Analysis of language. Some use of subject terminology. AO2
7. Contrasting ideas are used effectively, but would be strengthened by a quotation and analysis. AO1
8. Considering the effect on the audience. AO2
9. Wording could be improved but this is an effective use of visual stagecraft to support language details. Some subject terminology. AO2
10. Clear analysis of language, using subject terminology. AO2
11. Exploring contradictions, with a clear link back to the question. AO1
12. Useful link to context. Would be improved by making a link to the Headmaster's competitive attitude rather than the anachronism of the 1980s setting. AO3
13. Confident idea, although it would be useful to include a quotation or language analysis. AO1
14. Conclusion is decisive but balances different ideas together. The writing is competent and effective but sometimes the fluency could be improved. AO1/AO4

Questions

EXAM PRACTICE

Choose a paragraph of this essay, read it through a few times then try to improve it. You might:

- Replace a reference with a quotation.
- Analyse a quotation in more depth, including terminology.
- Improve the range of analysis of methods.
- Improve the expression, or sophistication of the vocabulary.
- Connect more context to the analysis.

Grade 7+ Annotated Response

A proportion of the best top-band answers will be awarded Grade 8 or Grade 9. To achieve this, you should aim for a sophisticated, fluid and nuanced response that displays flair and originality.

How does Bennett use the character of Hector to explore ideas about education?

Write about:

- how Bennett presents the character of Hector
- how Bennett uses Hector to explore some of his ideas.   [30 marks + 4 AO4 marks]

Through Hector, Bennett explores different attitudes to teaching. Hector's style is **idiosyncratic** and relies on his personal relationship with the boys (1). Other characters describe his methods as 'old-fashioned' and 'unquantifiable' (2), which, by the time Bennett was writing in 2004, was problematic as schools were increasingly judged on their league-table performance – which is the Headmaster's focus (3). Through the contrast between Hector's style and Irwin's, Bennett questions the best way to teach and what education is for (4).

Bennett's introduction of Hector demonstrates the respect of the boys and their close relationship as they remove his motorcycle leathers, naming the items in French (5). Their closeness is emphasised when Hector tells them they have a 'pact. Bread broken in secret'. This allusion to the Bible, one of many literary references, contradicts modern expectations (6) and suggests Hector's unusual methods. The 'pact' is further presented in the French scene. Bennett uses farce in the physical comedy of the boys, mid-brothel scene, being caught by the Headmaster. The visual comedy of the boys, acting a scene that could be interpreted as both brothel _and_ field hospital, puts Hector, the boys and the audience in opposition to the Headmaster, who is made to look foolish.

Bennett creates tension between Hector and Irwin's methods, as they argue about the purpose of education (7). Irwin uses the noun 'gobbets', contrasting with Hector's description of poetry learned 'by heart', **epitomising** their differences: Irwin wants to use the quotes to present a more interesting argument whereas Hector wants them as private comfort (8). However, an audience might feel Hector is being unfair to the boys in telling them they shouldn't use his teaching to pass exams – the reason they are there is to pass the Oxbridge exam, which Bennett took in the 1950s. Mrs Lintott also disagrees with Hector's methods:

Mrs Lintott: Do you think Hector is a good teacher? You see, I probably don't. (9)

Her close friendship with Hector is evident in the **adverb** 'probably', implying she isn't certain, but she argues that he is teaching the boys for 'inevitable failure', to have a comforting quotation rather than an exam qualification.

Bennett characterises Hector's teaching as being for life, not qualifications. He tells them 'we're making your deathbeds', a morbid image highlighting the age difference between teacher and student (10). Discussing 'Drummer Hodge', Hector says the best times in reading are 'as if a hand has come out and taken yours'. This simile suggests reading is comforting, but the stage direction suggests he reaches to Posner but <u>doesn't</u> touch him – there is almost comfort and connection, but something falls short. Perhaps literature does the same. Posner says to Irwin that Hector would see literature as 'medicine, wisdom, elastoplast. Everything'. His triadic structure is summed up in the final single word clause, emphasising how important literature is. Yet the final word of the three – 'elastoplast' – uses the symbol of something that goes over a wound, rather than healing it, as Posner doubts that literature is enough. Interestingly, despite usually being a counterpoint to Hector's ideas, Irwin almost contradicts Posner here as when he relates the conversation to Mrs Lintott he tells her he wanted to say, on the subject of homosexuality being a passing phase, that '<u>the</u> literature might say it does but that <u>literature</u> doesn't'. Here, Irwin uses the **determiner** to suggest that literature is indeed something that we can learn life lessons from, and take comfort from in similar experiences.

Hector's 'fondling' of the boys undermines his credibility and therefore his teaching methods. Bennett's decision to kill Hector at the end of the play suggests there is 'no room for his kind of teaching any more' but as Irwin also leaves the teaching profession, it's ambiguous as to what should replace it. Dakin's synthesis of the two styles, his 'subjunctive history', seems to be the new alternative as he's the younger generation. However, in the memorial service, Bennett celebrates Hector's life and contribution, suggesting regret that the education system pushes more towards the Headmaster and less towards the love of learning that Hector wanted to pass on (11).

1. The introduction establishes attitudes to education. AO1
2. Embedded, relevant quotation. AO2
3. Link to social contexts. AO3
4. Reference to contrasts, showing understanding of different attitudes. AO1/AO2
5. Analysis of stagecraft exploring Hector's role. AO2
6. Hector's teaching linked to social context. AO3
7. Focus on writer's methods by using Bennett's name to explore technique. AO1/AO2
8. Embedded, contrasting quotations with some evaluation of their meaning. AO2
9. Slightly longer quotation put on a new line for clarity. AO1
10. Analysis of stagecraft and language. AO2
11. Conclusion to the essay is well written with some precise sophisticated language. AO4

Questions

EXAM PRACTICE

Spend 45 minutes writing an answer to the following question. Remember to use the plan you have already prepared.

How does Bennett use the character of Irwin to explore ideas about education?

Write about:
- how Bennett presents the character of Irwin
- how Bennett uses Irwin to explore some of his ideas.

[30 marks + 4 AO4 marks]

Planning a Theme Question Response

You must be able to: understand what an exam question is asking you and prepare your response.

How might an exam question on a theme be phrased?

It will usually look like this:

How does Bennett explore disillusionment in *The History Boys*?

Write about:

- how different characters represent ideas of disillusionment
- how Bennett presents these ideas in the ways that he writes.

[30 marks + 4 AO4 marks]

How do I work out what to do?

Work out the focus of the question. In this case, it is about disillusionment – a sense of disappointment or failure – but there is also further guidance to lead you to write about the way this is represented through different characters. In answering thematic questions, it is useful to think: 'Which characters are mainly used to explore this theme? How do they contrast with one another?' and address the question that way.

'How' and 'why' are important elements. For AO1, you need to show understanding of the way that Hector teaches, and what other characters think about his methods.

For AO2, the word 'how' means you need to analyse the way that Bennett's use of language, structure and the dramatic form contribute to the audience's interpretation of disillusionment in the play, as seen through different characters. Ideally you should have quoted evidence, but you can make clear reference to specific parts of the play if necessary.

You also need to remember to link your answer to context to achieve AO3 marks and write accurately to gain the four AO4 marks for spelling, punctuation and grammar.

How do I plan my essay?

You have approximately 45 minutes to answer this question.

Although it doesn't seem long, spending the first five minutes writing a quick plan helps to focus your thoughts and produce a well-structured essay, an essential part of AO1.

Try to think of five or six ideas. Each of these can become a paragraph.

You can plan however you find most useful: a list, spider diagram or flow chart. Once you have your ideas, take a moment to check which order you want to write them in.

Look at the example of a spider diagram on the opposite page.

Audience disillusionment with Hector – is he a good teacher?
(Context: changing attitudes to professional relationships)
(Stagecraft: Hector's entrance/the memorial service 'ghost' appearance)

Hector's response to teaching – his enthusiasm and secret pact at the beginning, contrasted with his advice to Irwin at the end to leave teaching
(Context: changes in education)

How is disillusionment presented?

Posner's fate, described by Mrs Lintott; accepting Hector's teaching but unsuccessful
(Structure: opening Act 2 as 'Man')

Hector/Posner – *Drummer Hodge*
'Un-kissed. Un-rejoicing.'
(Stage direction: on Posner's knee)

Summary

- Make sure you understand the focus of the question (AO1).
- Analyse the way the writer conveys ideas through use of language, structure and form (AO2).
- Link ideas to social and historical context (AO3).
- Spell accurately, and use ambitious, precise vocabulary (AO4).

Questions

QUICK TEST
1. What key skills do you need to include in your answer?
2. What timings should you use?
3. Why is planning important?

EXAM PRACTICE
Plan a response to the following exam question:
How does Bennett present ideas about ageing and growing up?
Write about:
- how Bennett uses different characters to explore ideas about getting older
- how Bennett presents these ideas in the ways that he writes.
[30 marks + 4 AO4 marks]

How does Bennett explore disillusionment in *The History Boys*?

Write about:

- how different characters represent ideas of disillusionment
- how Bennett presents these ideas in the ways that he writes.

[30 marks + 4 AO4 marks]

Through the play, the characters of Hector and Posner are more disillusioned than any other characters. Hector is disillusioned with teaching and the audience is disillusioned with him because of the way he has been groping the boys. Posner takes his education seriously, but by the end of the play he has left Cambridge and lives alone, and could be considered the least successful of the boys (1).

Hector is obviously disillusioned when he puts his head on the desk and tells the boys that there is 'nothing of me left' (2). This is the same as an earlier action when he jokingly does the same thing. By the second time, the Headmaster has asked him to leave because of his inappropriate relationships with the boys. The boys don't know how to react and an audience will feel uncomfortable, as they can see how unhappy he is, and that he feels like he has wasted his life. He also tells Irwin he doesn't like himself as a teacher anymore (3). He describes his teaching as 'clowning', this verb suggests that he is focussed on the performance of his teaching instead of the importance of what he is teaching, and that it isn't taken seriously (4). Throughout the play, Irwin and Hector have conflicting views on how and what to teach. This reflects the changing expectations of education in the 1980s when the play is set, and 2004 when Bennett wrote 'The History Boys' (5). Hector is also disillusioned because of his relationship with the Headmaster who calls his type of teaching 'unquantifiable'. This word shows that the Headmaster values statistics and league tables, and Hector's teaching is too unpredictable for his liking (6).

The audience can also see Hector's disillusionment when he is reading 'Drummer Hodge' with Posner. They focus on the line 'Un-kissed. Un-rejoicing.' The use of the prefix 'un' makes the words very negative (7), which reflects Hector's negative feelings about his relationships and his teaching career as this comes straight after he has been asked to leave. Hector is feeling miserable and lonely (8). There is a stage direction which says Hector might put his hand on Posner's knee but doesn't. This shows the audience the connection between them that neither of them really talk about, that the audience also saw earlier when Posner was the one who comforted Hector. This creates a similarity between them that links them in the audience's mind (9).

Posner is also disillusioned by the end of the play as he hasn't achieved what he is learning how to do. Although he gets into Cambridge he doesn't stay there. At the beginning of Act 2, he approaches Irwin. In the stage directions, he's called 'Man', which removes his identity, and the audience might find his behaviour shocking as he's manipulating Irwin, which is different to how he behaved when at school when the audience is sympathetic to him. He tells Irwin that he didn't finish Cambridge.

'I thought I'd got somewhere, then I found I had to go on'. This quote shows how sad he is, because it creates an impression of loneliness and suggests that he is uncertain what to do next (10). This links to Alan Bennett's experience of education because he also went to Cambridge and then felt out of place a lot of the time (11).

At the end of the play, Mrs Lintott describes what happens to Posner, and he is a lonely person. He has online friends who don't really know who he is. She says that he 'haunts' the local library. This verb makes him sound like he is dead, not alive, and suggests that he doesn't have any purpose, that he is drifting around.

In some ways, Hector and Posner are very similar characters. They both are lonely and have trouble making good relationships with other people. They both experience disillusionment, because they are not able to do what they set out to do. Hector can't teach any more and Posner leaves Cambridge. They both lost hope in what they wanted (12).

1. A clear introduction, establishing the response to the question. AO1
2. Embedded quotation, which would be improved by analysis of language. AO1
3. Although phrasing could be improved, this is an insightful comment on character. AO1
4. Analysis of language using subject terminology. AO2
5. Reference to context, although in a general way. AO3
6. Analysis of language. AO2
7. Close language analysis with embedded subject terminology. AO2
8. Clear understanding of the effect of language. AO1/AO2
9. This paragraph creates a transition in the essay to the second character. Although it could be more clearly expressed, it's focussed on audience response and analyses stagecraft. AO1/AO2
10. Explanation of effect on the audience. AO2
11. Brief reference to context. Accurate but could be more fluently expressed. AO3
12. Conclusion summarises the point and brings it back to the question. The essay is clear and structured, although the phrasing could be improved with more sophisticated language. AO1/AO4

Questions

EXAM PRACTICE
Choose a paragraph of this essay, read it through a few times then try to improve it. You might:
- Replace a reference with a quotation.
- Analyse a quotation in more depth, including terminology.
- Improve the range of analysis of methods.
- Improve the expression, or sophistication of the vocabulary.
- Connect more context to the analysis.

Grade 7+ Annotated Response

A proportion of the best top-band answers will be awarded Grade 8 or Grade 9. To achieve this, you should aim for a sophisticated, fluid and nuanced response that displays flair and originality.

How does Bennett explore disillusionment in *The History Boys*? Write about:

- how different characters represent ideas of disillusionment
- how Bennett presents these ideas in the ways that he writes.

[30 marks + 4 AO4 marks]

Bennett presents disillusionment through his characterisation of Hector and Posner (1). Hector's relationship with the boys changes and he recognises a change in himself at the end of his career. Posner experiences disillusionment through his lack of fulfilment, seen in the final description of his future.

The audience sees Hector's disillusionment develop. Early in the play, this is foreshadowed when Hector 'sits with his head on the desk, a parody of despair'. This stage direction is echoed when Hector despairs that there is 'nothing of me left' (2) after the Headmaster has confronted and dismissed him over his groping the boys. The boys respond awkwardly, unable to distinguish between parody and reality. The audience feels a similar discomfort at this revelation of a teacher in the classroom: a taboo being broken (3). The audience becomes further disillusioned with Hector as his groping is further revealed. Although it's obvious from the beginning in Scripps and Dakin's conversation, when Hector is confronted he refuses to acknowledge his inappropriate behaviour, instead dismissing it with a quotation that can come across as flippant. Bennett has said in interviews that the boys are over-age and more mature than Hector. However, a modern audience with a different attitude to the responsibilities of adults in authority, particularly after increasingly publicised allegations of historic abuse, could view Hector as even more guilty and irresponsible (4).

The conflict between Hector and Irwin's teaching styles contributes to Hector's disillusionment. Hector admits he wanted the boys 'to show off, to come up with the short answer ... I wanted them to compete'. His language of presentation conforms to Irwin's journalistic style of teaching, rather than Hector's professed goal of providing the boys with an education for life – to have 'the antidote ready. Grief. Happiness'. Hector's use of single-noun emotions focusses on the medicinal side of literature, exposed by Posner as inadequate when he goes to Irwin rather than Hector for advice: 'Literature is medicine, wisdom, elastoplast. Everything. It isn't, though, is it, sir?' Posner's triadic structure suggests a sense of conflict as literature begins as medicine – healing and permanent – but ends as an elastoplast, covering over a wound, while his **rhetorical question** suggests he is disillusioned with Hector's all-encompassing belief in the power of literature (5). Hector's ideas about education are called old-fashioned and 'unquantifiable' by the Headmaster, who is influenced by league tables and the increasing competition between schools that developed through the 1980s and which was prevalent in 2004 when Bennett wrote the play, with league tables determining the reputation of schools (6).

Hector's disillusionment is evident in his conversation with Posner on 'Drummer Hodge'. He focusses on the negative prefixes of Hardy and Larkin – 'Un-kissed. Un-confessed ... Un-spent. Un-fingermarked'. Placing each in separate sentences heightens the sense of division; spoken onstage they would be slow-paced with pauses, as Hector comes to terms with his position (7). He is also expressing his closeted sexuality, recognising in the negatives a sense of 'not sharing, of being out of it ... Not being in the swim'. He shares this moment with Posner as it seems they will touch but once again the moment passes. However, considering their relative positions of authority, the audience might also be momentarily relieved at Hector's restraint.

Bennett also explores disillusionment through Posner's characterisation (8). At the opening of Act 2, he is simply 'Man', which hides his identity, although onstage he is presumably played by the same actor. Of all the boys, Posner's future is the least fulfilled (9). Having suffered a mental breakdown, he has left Cambridge despite his efforts to get there and, at the end, he lives alone, has few friends and 'haunts' the local library. This verb gives the impression that he is a ghost, half-alive without fulfilling a purpose.

Through his characterisation of Hector and Posner, Bennett presents disillusionment; they lack the fulfilment of their promise, and although they both experience some comfort in their knowledge of literature, they lack the real-world relationships necessary to lead emotionally fulfilling lives (10).

1. Establishes a clear line of argument, focussed on two characters. AO1
2. Fluent embedding of quotation linked with stagecraft. AO2
3. Close exploration of the effect on the audience. AO2
4. Developed reference to context, applied to the discussion. AO3
5. Specific language is explored in detail, with fluently embedded subject vocabulary. AO2
6. Embedded contextual reference linked to interpretation. AO3
7. Analysis of stagecraft and language closely addressing the question. AO1/AO2
8. Paragraphs always return to the main theme of the question. AO1
9. Evaluative comment on the play as a whole. AO1
10. Ends with a quick conclusion that is evaluative and, like the rest of the essay, is well-written with precise and sophisticated language. AO1/AO4

Questions

EXAM PRACTICE

Spend 45 minutes writing an answer to the following question. Remember to use the plan you have already prepared.

How does Bennett present ideas about ageing and growing up?

Write about:

- how Bennett uses different characters to explore ideas about getting older
- how Bennett presents these ideas in the ways that he writes.

[30 marks + 4 AO4 marks]

Glossary

Absurdity – something ridiculous or wildly unreasonable.

Adjective – a word that describes a noun.

Adverb – a word that describes a verb.

Allusion – a reference to something else, often literary.

Anachronistic – belonging to a period that isn't the one being portrayed.

Aside – a remark in the play intended to be heard by the audience, but not other characters.

Bias – inclination for or against a group of people, usually unfair.

Clause – a grammatical unit; a section of a sentence.

Cliché – an overused phrase, which lacks original thought.

Climax – the most intense part of an act or the whole play.

Colloquialism – everyday slang word.

Confidant – a person who shares a secret or private matter.

Conflict – a disagreement or argument.

Congruent – in agreement or harmony.

Contradictory – opposed or inconsistent.

Counterpoint – forming a notable contrast.

Declarative – a statement.

Determiner – a word referencing a noun, e.g. a, an, the, every.

Disingenuous – not sincere or honest; pretending to know less about something.

Dramatic irony – when the audience of a play is aware of something that a character on stage isn't.

Echoing – repeating an idea from earlier in the narrative.

Elitist – believing society should be run by a group of superior ability or quality to the rest of society.

Emotive – creating or describing strong emotions.

Emphatic – expressing something forcibly and clearly.

Epitomising – to be a perfect example of.

Esoteric – likely to be understood by only a small number of people, with specialist knowledge.

Euphemistic – using a mild or indirect way of saying something unpleasant.

Extended metaphor – a comparison that continues for several lines, scenes, or longer.

Farce – a style of comedy entertaining through absurdity, physical humour and improbable situations.

Fatalistic – believing that all events are predetermined, therefore inevitable.

Flamboyant – attracting attention because of exuberant, excessive behaviour.

Flash-forward – a dramatic device taking a play forwards in time.

Foil – a character contrasting with another.

Foreshadows – hint at future events in the play.

Glossing – to explain or give a definition.

Hyperbole – exaggeration to emphasise an idea.

Hypocritical – claiming to have better standards or behaviour than is true.

Idiom – a colloquial phrase with a figurative, rather than a literal, meaning.

Idiosyncratic – a manner of behaviour of thought specific to an individual.

Imperative – an order.

Incredulous – unwilling or unable to believe something.

Innuendo – a remark that is subtly suggestive.

Interjection – a short expression of emotion.

Irony – something that seems the opposite of what was expected; deliberately using words that mean the opposite of what is intended.

Juxtapose – place or deal with close together for contrasting effect.

Marginalised – a person, group or idea treated as insignificant.

Melancholy – a feeling of thoughtful sadness.

Meretricious – attractive but falsely showy, with little value.

Metaphor – a descriptive technique, using comparison to say one thing is something else.

Meta-theatre – aspects of a play that call attention to its fictional nature as drama or theatre.

Narrator – someone telling the story, or delivering a commentary alongside.

Noun – a word to identify any of a type of people, places, or things (common noun), or to name a particular one of these (proper noun).

Paradox – a statement difficult to understand because it includes two opposing facts or characteristics.

Parallelism – repeating similar word orders or sentence constructions to emphasise an idea.

Physical comedy – comedy focussed on manipulating the body for humorous effect.

Pragmatic – sensible, rational and practical.

Prefix – a word or part of word placed before another, for example, un-, de-, re-, mis-.

Protagonist – the main character in a work of fiction.

Renaissance man – a person with many talents or areas of knowledge.

Rhetoric – language designed to have a persuasive or impressive effect.

Rhetorical question – a question asked in order to create thought rather than to get a specific answer.

Sacrilegious – misuse of what is regarded as sacred.

Sarcastic – using irony to mock.

Sardonic – bitter or scornful tone.

Self-deprecating – to be modest or critical of oneself, especially for comic purposes.

Semantic field – a series of connected words.

Simile – a descriptive technique, using comparison to say one thing is 'like' or 'as' something else.

Stage directions – instructions in a script indicating movement, position or tone of an actor, or staging including sound, lighting and scenery.

Stichomythia – lines in a play alternating between two characters but repeating certain words to emphasise specific ideas.

Subjunctive – a verb form expressing possibility.

Sympathy – to have sympathy with; to have an understanding between people.

Synthesis – combining elements to form a connected whole.

Taboo language – words and phrases considered inappropriate in certain contexts.

Tragic – extreme suffering, distress or sorrow.

Transition – a period of change from one condition to another.

Triadic structure – a group of three closely related words, phrases or ideas.

Unrequited – not returned.

Verb phrase – a verb combined with another word to convey mood, tense or person.

Answers

destruction of his career. Analysis could include the following: the semantic fields of sadness or emotion; Dakin's short fragmented sentences and staging of these; Irwin's triadic structure suggesting the passage of time; Hector's emotive final speech and the connection between him and Posner in light of the flash-forwards earlier in the Act.

Pages 4–5

Quick Test

1. Different interpretations of its value – some universities being more or less respected. The different nature of Hector and Irwin's teaching.
2. Mrs Lintott – facts and accuracy are paramount. The Headmaster wants more presentational flair to be impressive.
3. Sarcastic and comic. He's one of the boys' leaders, confident and self-aware (so far). He's dismissive of Irwin. Posner's in love with him, but he's dating Fiona.
4. Protective of Hector but inappropriately so (the French scene, the bike). Suspicious of Irwin but mostly giving him a chance as he's saying something new.

Exam Practice

Answers might include the following: the conflict of facts versus presentation; accuracy not being enough; the teaching of Irwin being about shock and strategy contrasted with Lintott's thorough facts and Hector's variety; the role of league tables in shaping educational curricula.

Pages 6–7

Quick Test

1. Henry VIII to understand Stalin, Hitler and Margaret Thatcher.
2. He misses the clear facts of Mrs Lintott. Irwin's lessons are 'flavour' and 'cutting edge'.
3. To equip the boys for understanding emotional situations: grief, happiness and so on.
4. Dakin's dating Fiona, the headmaster's secretary and his 'Western Front'. Posner's in love with Dakin.
5. He's baffled/confused that they say they won't use it in an exam, and sees it as the perfect way to conclude an essay or conduct an argument.

Exam Practice

Answers might include Irwin's use of angles/back door/ window approach compared with Hector's far-off future (both different to the traditional view given by Mrs Lintott). Analysis could consider the medical term 'antidote' linked with death, the extended metaphor Rudge uses or the short juxtaposed declaratives from Akthar summarising the two approaches.

Pages 8–9

Quick Test

1. He knows Irwin also looks at Dakin and wants companionship. He fears Hector will only offer a quotation.
2. Irwin's changed the way he thinks. There's some hero-worship and he wants Irwin to think him clever.
3. The Headmaster's wife saw him, on the motorbike, from the charity shop where she volunteers.
4. Hector has to share lessons with Irwin and should consider early retirement. When Hector responds with poetry the Headmaster becomes angry and swears at him.
5. They share *Drummer Hodge* and the consolation to be found in poetry. In the moment of melancholy, it seems as if Hector will touch Posner's knee but doesn't.

Exam Practice

Answers might include the discussion of literature as consolation, Posner's desire for comfort or the discovery/ censure of Hector's actions along with the potential

Pages 10–11

Quick Test

1. Posner. He's dropped out of Cambridge and, on advice from his therapist, is selling a story about Irwin to a newspaper.
2. Awkwardness. Posner tries to comfort him, Scripps and Dakin sit back, feeling disturbed by Hector's openness.
3. That he's insuring the boys against failure rather than trying to help them achieve.
4. Hector believes the boys should condemn it as an atrocity. Irwin does think there's room to find an angle. But both tell Dakin he's pushing it too far – Irwin too has a line that shouldn't be crossed.

Exam Practice

Answers could include Mrs Lintott's fears on lack of achievement, how far Hector's teaching career could be considered a failure or the Headmaster's conflict between quantifiable exam results and Hector's education for life. Analysis could consider the logical, almost scientific, language of the Headmaster, Mrs Lintott's use of the word 'insurance', Hector's taboo language in front of the boys and his curt dismissive imperative 'go away'.

Pages 12–13

Quick Test

1. Posner tells Scripps he loves Dakin, but that he's also noticed Irwin watching Dakin.
2. 'One fucking thing after another', the taboo language suggesting his distaste for the process of logic and narrative applied to it.
3. 'History is women following behind with the bucket', implying that women are usually clearing up after men's mess.
4. Because Dakin's use of Hector's lessons to come up with 'subjunctive history' shows he's synthesised what he's learned with both teachers to develop his own ideas.

Exam Practice

Answers might include the following: the different interpretations of history the teachers have; the discussions about presentation, truth and fact during the interviews; Dakin's comments on subjunctive history. Analysis might include Irwin's doubtful subordinate clause 'provided, of course', the comparison of Posner to 'spaniel', the animal metaphor suggesting loyalty that won't, contrary to Scripp's suggestion, pass and Hector's frustrated questioning.

Pages 14–15

Quick Test

1. Scripps goes to Eucharist, remembers himself as naive and idealistic. Dakin looks for evidence of Irwin. Posner is isolated, but loves the architecture.
2. Rudge is admitted partly because his father used to work there. However, he also performed in the interview and he is what they're looking for in the sports teams.
3. The Headmaster tells him to take Irwin instead of Dakin, who had volunteered.
4. The Headmaster gives a eulogy, although it's a bit hypocritical, and Mrs Lintott tells the audience what happens to the boys. Hector speaks directly to them about what he wanted them to learn.

Exam Practice

Answers might include the following: the accident solving the question of Irwin's wheelchair; death as a final choice, rather than Hector being either fired or having a reprieve from losing his job; the memorial service, with the stories about what the boys have achieved creating a sense of closure; the final statements about education from the boys and teachers. Analysis might consider Posner's unexpected swearing and direct statement of desire with the additional

age direction; Scripps' quotation referring to Irwin/Dakin's
arlier 'subjunctive history' conversation and Scripps' role as a
arrator; the Headmaster's clichéd metaphors; Hector's final
mperatives, short and focussed – a dual instruction to them
nd the audience.

ages 16–17

uick Test

1. They transition or overlap, without a clean break.
2. By using comedy, for example, the Headmaster or Rudge, to counterpoint more serious scenes.
3. Knowledge of Irwin's wheelchair casts a shadow over the play, with the audience waiting for an accident to happen.
4. Dramatic irony, pointing out the unreal nature of theatre, and shapes the audience's response to events.

xam Practice

nswers might include the use of comedy or Scripps' narration
 guide the reader's emotion and create dramatic irony.
nalysis might include the echo of 'rattled' from earlier in the
lay, creating a fearful foreshadowing, or the use of meta-
heatre to comment on the play's storyline.

ages 18–19

uick Test

1. In Leeds, Yorkshire, in the 1940s/1950s.
2. Characters with a sarcastic or dark sense of humour, that become resigned to difficult situations.
3. The practical down-to-earth nature of the boys and their black humour regarding Hector's paedophilic actions.

xam Practice

omments might include the belief several teachers express
at they can't go to somewhere like Oxbridge and should
ettle' for an alternative university, less academic and
restigious (perhaps mentioning the irony of several teachers
pplying to but not attending Oxbridge themselves). Lower
xpectations of Rudge, who gets in anyway, and the idea that
ey won't be happy at Oxford because they won't fit in.

ages 20–21

uick Test

1. Bennett's own, including his university application; the 1980s when the play is set; 2004 when the play was written.
2. Out of place among independently educated students, not confident in his comparative abilities and in awe of the building he was in.
3. Introduction of league tables to rank schools on results, creating a marketplace-style competition.
4. Posner: admires the architecture, then feels it's impossible to fit in (although Bennett did graduate); Hector: he confuses the smell of cold stone and learning, and thinks he wouldn't have learned the difference at Oxford.

xam Practice

omments might include the Headmaster's reasons linked
ith the changes made in the 1980s/1990s to education and
e way the Headmaster thinks more about the appearance of
e school – attracting students/parents to apply – rather than
e welfare of individual current students. Elsewhere in the
lay, he uses the school photograph as publicity rather than
cording a memory, and wants a full set of scholarships for
e prestige of achieving it, rather than feeling sympathy for
udge (when he thinks Rudge hasn't had an offer).

ages 22–23

uick Test

1. Posner and Scripps, although most of the boys sing at some point.
2. 'Bewitched, Bothered and Bewildered' by Ella Fitzgerald.
3. It's the most contemporary song, suggesting the difference between the boys and Hector, as the boys leave.
4. Their detachment from 1980s youth culture; the influence Hector has had on them and their separation from the other boys.

Exam Practice

Ideas might include the ways that music underlines the
emotions, either to heighten/explain it (frequently Posner) or
to create contrast (the memorial/waving goodbye). Emotions
might be explored further in the lyrics, e.g. 'the laugh's on me'
suggests how helpless Posner is, and his fear of being ridiculed
by the other boys for his unrequited love for Dakin. Answers
might also explore the dramatic presentation of music during
scene changes to maintain pace.

Pages 24–25

Quick Test

1. A style of comedy characterised by physical and verbal humour, unlikely or improbable situations and mistaken identity.
2. Use of farce including physical humour through the dual interpretations of the boys, the misunderstanding of the Headmaster and the interruption of Irwin.
3. To cover scene changes and to provide additional background scenes, for example, Dakin and Fiona.
4. Creates dramatic irony by looking back on the play's events from a future time. Uses meta-theatre to comment on the expectations of story-telling.

Exam Practice

Ideas might include the following: the use of farce and
physical theatre in the war zone/brothel comparison; the
interruption of Irwin clearly understanding more French than
the Headmaster – as a possible moment of discovery (how
much does he understand?); the 'moment' indicating tension,
fear of discovery and perhaps resentment into
the relationship between Hector and the boys.

Pages 26–27

Quick Test

1. As being for life, not just for passing exams.
2. Warm and affectionate, although eventually resents the 'waste' of his life in a school. He takes advantage of their relationship when giving them lifts home.
3. As slightly patronising, preparing the boys for failure.
4. As unpredictable and unquantifiable.
5. He dies in a motorbike accident while giving Irwin a lift home.

Exam Practice

Answers could include that he's arguably the **protagonist**
of the play, his death being the central focus of the play's
climax, the pitiful nature of the end of his career. Analysis
could focus on his use of the 'un' prefix suggesting his failure,
the language of missed opportunities (negative language),
his relationship with Posner with the short declarative or the
emphatic 'by heart'.

Pages 28–29

Quick Test

1. Government media strategist, on-screen historian and teacher.
2. He uses performance and presentation to 'mist the windows' and shape arguments.
3. Dakin propositions him; Irwin eventually accepts but the accident means Dakin never follows through.
4. Not to touch Dakin. He also says not to stay in teaching.

Exam Practice

Answers could include the change in Irwin over time, the use
of presentation and showiness to hide or change the truth
and the challenge of an argument becoming more attractive
than the truth. Analysis might consider Irwin's frequent
use of metaphor, the quotation of liberty/freedom with its
paradoxical message, the short declaratives that demonstrates
Irwin's understanding of rhetoric, the list Dakin employs and
the **innuendo** in Irwin's acceptance of Dakin's proposition.

Answers

Quick Test
1. Good results and the reputation the school can get from them.
2. They're unquantifiable and unpredictable.
3. In the French scene, very awkwardly. Mostly he's seen with teachers not students. He rearranges the photograph for the school's benefit not the boys' memories.

Exam Practice
Answers might include his desire for results, putting the school above the boys and his concern for education and presentation to create an impression. Analysis might include the metaphor of money in his eulogy, contrary to Hector's beliefs, and his repeated use of 'quantify' and similar mathematical vocabulary. Analysis might also include the comparison of boys with animals or the short **parallelism** of the declarative contrasting with the importance of boys/school.

Pages 38–39
Quick Test
1. His detachment from others, lack of joking about sex but careful listening instead. He can thoughtfully advise and question.
2. That he believes strongly, but he views his beliefs with detachment and thinks he might grow out of them.
3. His father was a college servant, he's good at sports, and has learned the same subject content and interview skills as the other boys.
4. He owns a company building affordable homes for first-time buyers.

Exam Practice
Answers might include the following: the narrative role of Scripps setting him apart from the other boys but acting as the audience's 'voice'; Scripps' relationships with Dakin and Posner; Rudge's role as comic voice and as a blunt, honest student. Analysis might include Scripps' interjections at different points in the play, giving his comment 'love apart' the weight of authority as well as its declarative nature, or his self-deprecating humour with the simile suggesting that faith is linked with social trends/fashions. Analysis might also include Rudge's bluntness about others' perceptions of his intellect, the taboo language playing up to expectations and his challenging tone in contradicting Mrs Lintott's assessment of him.

Pages 40–41
Quick Test
1. Akthar, Muslim; Timms, class clown; Crowther, actor; Lockwood, acts in the classroom scenes.
2. Using an extended metaphor of war. She's used first to show Dakin's attitude to sex (as he talks to Scripps about her) and then he uses his relationship to get Hector's job back.
3. She is an unseen, relatively insignificant character in her own right, used by men (Dakin, the Headmaster, Hector – although unknowingly) to achieve their purposes.

Exam Practice
Answers might include using Fiona as a device to explore the boys' developing sexuality and their merging of history with their everyday, present, experiences, using the extended metaphors. Analysis might also include the role of the minor student characters to create comedy in the classroom scenes, with their quick-paced witty banter.

Pages 42–43
Quick Test
1. Irwin focusses on exams, Hector on cultural education, which he says is irrelevant to exams.
2. That education can overcome social barriers and that not teaching all students the same content, in the same way, can be patronising.
3. Qualifications and results, which push a school up the league table.
4. They combine the two approaches to teaching history –

Pages 30–31
Quick Test
1. At first, he dismisses him as too young and inexperienced, trying to impress them. Then he begins to hero-worship him, trying to impress Irwin, inviting him for a drink and sex.
2. As another game, something to be enjoyed as much as possible (unlike Posner).
3. Mostly he ignores Posner's crush on him but, at the end, he embraces him fully.
4. By blackmailing the Headmaster over his attempts to 'feel up Fiona'.

Exam Practice
Answers could explore Dakin's changing relationship with Irwin, including the disappointment/rejection in the stage direction and line breaks implying his let-down or his use of taboo language to show his anger. Answers might also include his relationships with the boys as their leader, or Fiona with the extended metaphor of battle reflecting his lack of empathy.

Pages 32–33
Quick Test
1. Dakin
2. He's gay and Jewish. He's also the most sensitive of the boys in many ways.
3. Singing to emphasise the emotion of scenes and glossing definitions to move between scenes. Some dark comedy, for example, Posner's hopelessness.
4. He dropped out of Cambridge and lives alone, looking for news of the boys' achievements. He tries to write a newspaper article about what happened at the school.

Exam Practice
Answers might include discussion of Posner as an outsider and his unrequited love for Dakin, and make reference to the sadness of his ending in Mrs Lintott's description. Analysis might explore the word 'haunts', with its deathly connotations, and the frequent negatives used by Posner, or the language of fear suggesting his anxiety.

Pages 34–35
Quick Test
1. They've not had any power or authority – they stay in the background of important moments.
2. Affectionate, but she keeps a professional distance and doesn't try to be their friend.
3. She teaches History plainly, but thoroughly and extremely well.
4. She's frustrated and disapproving, but remains affectionate towards him – she sees him more as foolish than anything else.

Exam Practice
Answers could focus on Mrs Lintott's exploration of women's role in history and her dislike of their position. Analysis might include her comments on women retreating or having to clear up after men, along with her sarcastic tone and blunt honesty. Some answers might include an alternative argument about Bennett's focus on male characters at Lintott's expense or the lack of influence she ultimately has.

they are successful in exams but also value the wider emotional and social lessons from Hector.

Exam Practice

Answers might include the conflict of exams and lifelong learning, and who favours which approach. Analysis could consider Hector's frequent literary allusions, his alliterative **hyperbole** 'enemy of education', the language of purpose/the future.

Pages 44–45

Quick Test

1. Hector requires absorption or culture, and insists it's not for an exam. Irwin focusses on exam-based discussion and essay writing to develop presentation of an argument.
2. Rudge relies on writing down specific interpretations; he sometimes finds the discussion-based lessons difficult.
3. She taught thoroughly and factually: the boys achieved very highly with her.

Exam Practice

Answers might include the diverse styles, linking to the different values of education expressed by different characters; also consider the way the boys respond differently to the teachers. Analysis might include Rudge's extended metaphor of battery farming, Irwin's use of metaphor to describe essay writing or Timms' joking manner identifying key differences between Hector and Irwin's effect on the class.

Pages 46–47

Quick Test

1. To highlight or emphasise emotions onstage, or discuss key themes of the play.
2. Their homosexuality foreshadows the hidden sexualities of Hector, Posner and Irwin.
3. To prevent the boys becoming too reverent, to make literature everyday 'pop culture' as well.
4. As joy (Scripps), consolation (Dakin) and baffling (Timms).

Exam Practice

Ideas might include the value all characters place on literature and the conflict between Hector's insistence on it as personal and private contrasted with Irwin's exam techniques, and Mrs Lintott's expectation that cultural knowledge contributes to competing economically. Analysis might include the emotional language associated with literature, the contrasts of joy/consolation, the language of empathy and companionships associated with literature.

Pages 48–49

Quick Test

1. He teaches 'angles' and presentation, as he does as a TV journalist and media strategist, designing his arguments to be persuasive.
2. As facts, logical and connected, without bias.
3. That people impose narratives on history, making it into a story, whereas Rudge describes history as disconnected – one thing after another.
4. That everything should be open to interpretation and those who win or have power tend to write the story of their history.

Exam Practice

Answers might include the conflict between Mrs Lintott and Irwin, played out through the boys. Analysis might consider the gendered argument of Mrs Lintott – just as valid and therefore perhaps a synthesis of Irwin and Lintott's teaching would be the best approach. Analysis could also consider the language of storytelling and narrative, as well as biased language.

Pages 50–51

Quick Test

1. Dakin calls Hitler a statesman and argues to see the Holocaust in context; Irwin sees that as taking his teaching to 'find an angle' too far.
2. Irwin mostly doesn't discuss truth as being objective; everything for him is subject to different arguments and interpretations.

3. Hector says the boys should tell the truth, looking for the central honesty in their ideas, but his personal behaviour doesn't always demonstrate the same.
4. She teachers facts without presentation or biased interpretation.

Exam Practice

Analysis might include the use of rhetorical questions related to truth prompting discussion, the difference between truth and point of view, or Irwin's comparative suggesting that truth is irrelevant; persuasive presentation and entertainment is more important.

Pages 52–53

Quick Test

1. Posner, Hector, Irwin and Dakin
2. Dakin often boasts about it and frequently tells the boys about his 'progress'. Rudge confirms he is having sex, but only on Fridays to keep his weekend free for sport. He doesn't discuss his partners at all.
3. She refers to 'other things' she experienced for the first time at university, but in a dismissive tone.
4. He notices Posner's love for Dakin before Posner himself. He continues to be affectionate and Posner's closest friend. When Dakin decides to offer Irwin sex, Scripps says it's an inappropriate thank you gift.
5. That the boys are over the age of consent, and that Hector is more child-like and innocent than they are.

Exam Practice

Answers might include the struggles some characters have with sexuality and the prevalence of homosexuality in the characters. Analysis might consider the derogatory language casually used by the boys compared with the more violent language of the Headmaster; the flippant tone of 'scarred for life', which indicates the opposite, and the way that Posner seeks support in understanding his sexuality in different ways.

Pages 54–55

Quick Test

1. By giving them the sense that they're always able to find comfort or inspiration in someone else's experiences.
2. Mrs Lintott says he doesn't focus enough on the outcome of education or their career prospects. At the start, he encourages them to aim for less than Oxbridge.
3. He gets into Cambridge but then he has had a nervous breakdown, leaves university, is in therapy and struggles to make friends. Yet, he is also the only pupil who fully appreciates the broad education Hector offered.
4. By suggesting that the boys have good careers following the opportunities their education gives them and by describing Hector's teaching as 'the only education worth having'.

Exam Practice

Analysis could include the following: Mrs Lintott's critical tone in the noun 'droves' or 'notion'; Hector's use of the negatives in discussing the lack of belonging and sense of isolation, implicitly implying that community and relationships are the most important factors; Hector's triadic imperatives at the end insisting on the importance of a broader understanding of education.

Pages 56–57

Quick Test

1. Slightly patronising towards anywhere that isn't Oxbridge; his characters recognise them as being good but they're still not as good.
2. The boys are told to lower their expectations to something more realistic and the teachers express some surprise when they get in, particularly with Rudge's success. The boys all take on professional jobs by the end, and are described by Mrs Lintott as 'pillars of the community'.

Answers

3. He's bitter, maybe even resentful, that some students are taught and cultured differently – it could reflect his own attendance at Bristol rather than Oxford. He mentions their travels and education related to it, which places them in a stronger position because of their wider cultural knowledge and experiences.

Exam Practice

Answers could focus on the way that the boys are encouraged to lower their ambitions, in part because of their backgrounds and experiences. Some answers might also include ideas about education as being a leveller or key to social equality – Mrs Lintott's comment about children being artists or the teaching of wider culture from Hector and Irwin. Analysis might include Irwin's list of cultural destinations and his demeaning simile 'like thoroughbreds' using the analogy of horse-racing for children's achievement. Analysis might also include the colloquial language used by Rudge ('and all that').

Pages 60-61

Practice Questions

Use the mark scheme below to self-assess your strengths and weaknesses. The estimated grade boundaries are included so you can assess your progress towards your target grade.

Pages 62-63

Quick Test

1. AO1 focussed, structured answer to the character in question; AO2 – how Bennett uses language, structure and dramatic form to convey his ideas; AO3 – links to social, historical and theatrical context; AO4 – accurate spelling, punctuation and grammar.

2. 45 minutes to write, including around 5 minutes to plan.

3. To gather ideas and put them into an organised, coherent structure (AO1).

Exam Practice

Ideas might include the following: Irwin's exam-driven focus; his emphasis on education being for passing exams and getting qualifications rather than Hector's interpretation; Irwin's journalistic style, leading to his later jobs as government media strategist and TV historian. The way the boys integrate Irwin and Hector's different teaching styles.

Pages 66–67 and 72–73

Use the mark scheme below to self-assess your strengths and weaknesses. Work up from the bottom, putting a tick by things you have fully accomplished, a ½ by skills that are in place but need securing and underlining areas that need particular development. The estimated grade boundaries are included so you can assess your progress towards your target grade.

Pages 68–69

Quick Test

1. AO1 focussed, structured answer to the character in question; AO2 – how Bennett uses language, structure and dramatic form to convey his ideas; AO3 – links to social, historical and theatrical context; AO4 – accurate spelling, punctuation and grammar.

2. 45 minutes to write, including around 5 minutes to plan.

3. To gather ideas and put them into an organised, coherent structure (AO1).

Exam Practice

Ideas might include the following: the conflict between Hector – older, more experience – and Irwin – youthful, new, often referred to by the boys as being their age, with any similarities between Mrs Lintott's attitude and Hector's; the boys being between A-Levels and university, learning different ways to approach and think about ideas as they become more independent, moving from Mrs Lintott's teaching to Irwin's; the developing sexualities, especially Dakin and Posner; the way the boys must decide for themselves; the future impressions we have of the boys' lives at the end.

Grade	AO1 (12 marks)	AO2 (12 marks)	AO3 (6 marks)	AO4 (4 marks)
6–7+	A convincing, well-structured essay that answers the question fully. Quotations and references are well chosen and integrated into sentences. The response covers the whole play.	Analysis of the full range of Bennett's methods. Thorough exploration of the effects of these methods. Accurate range of subject terminology.	Exploration is linked to specific aspects of the play's contexts to show a detailed understanding.	Consistent high level of accuracy. Vocabulary and sentences are used to make ideas clear and precise.
4–5	A clear essay that always focusses on the exam question. Quotations and references support ideas effectively. The response refers to different points in the play.	Explanations of Bennet's different methods. Clear understanding of the effects of these methods. Accurate use of subject terminology.	References to relevant aspects of context to show a clear understanding.	Good level of accuracy. Vocabulary and sentences help to keep ideas clear.
2–3	The essay has some good ideas that are mostly relevant. Some quotations and references are used to support ideas.	Identification of some different methods used by Bennett to convey meaning. Some subject terminology.	Some awareness of how ideas in the play link to context.	Reasonable level of accuracy. Errors do not get in the way of the essay making sense.